Critical Guides to French Texts

74 Corneille: Le Cid

Critical Guides to French Texts

EDITED BY ROGER LITTLE, WOLFGANG VAN EMDEN,
DAVID WILLIAMS

CORNEILLE

Le Cid

W. D. Howarth

Emeritus Professor of Classical French Literature
University of Bristol

Grant & Cutler Ltd
1988

© Grant & Cutler Ltd
1988

ISBN 0-7293-0289-X

I.S.B.N. 84-599-2550-1

DEPÓSITO LEGAL: V. 2.706 - 1988

Printed in Spain by
Artes Gráficas Soler, S. A., Valencia

for

GRANT & CUTLER LTD
55-57, GREAT MARLBOROUGH STREET, LONDON W1V 2AY

Contents

CONTENTS

Introduction

A N Y O N E well versed in the history of European drama, if asked to pick out the essential characteristics of seventeenth-century French tragedy, will probably choose such features as its simplicity, concentration and unity of tone. If he has been brought up in the English theatrical tradition, he will no doubt have in mind an implicit contrast between French classical practice and that of Shakespeare and other Elizabethan dramatists. The best-known expression of this contrast for readers of an older generation remains Lytton Strachey's comparison of *Antony and Cleopatra* and *Bérénice*,[1] but though the extreme simplicity of the latter play makes it particularly suitable for the purpose of such a comparison, any other of Racine's tragedies would serve almost equally well – and not only any of Racine's, but any of Corneille's, from *Horace* (1640) to *Suréna* (1674). For while the numerous seventeenth– and eighteenth-century 'parallels' between these two playwrights certainly sought to distinguish between them in terms of psychological content and the nature of the tragic experience, there was never any doubt that the essential dramatic formula was the same; and from the time of their active rivalry in the 1660s and 1670s onwards, the names of Corneille and Racine have always been coupled as the supreme exponents of the art-form they developed and brought to perfection.

However, whereas Jean Racine, born in 1639, began writing for the theatre when what we call classical tragedy was

---

[1] *Landmarks in French Literature* (1912), London, Thornton Butterworth, 1936, pp. 93ff.

already well established (his first tragedy, *La Thébaïde,* dates
from 1664), Pierre Corneille was his senior by over thirty
years, and had made his debut as a playwright (at the age of
twenty-three) as early as 1629, at a time when the classical
aesthetic had scarcely been formulated, and had not yet
begun to impose itself on French playgoers; when the dominant theatrical style was still relatively free and undisciplined;
and when tragicomedy had not yet given way to tragedy as
the most popular dramatic genre. Although *Le Cid,* produced
during the theatrical season 1636-37, is often referred to as
the first major example of French classical tragedy – and
although its importance in the evolution of that genre cannot
be questioned – it was originally presented as a tragicomedy,
and was labelled 'tragicomédie' in the first edition, published
in 1637. Not the least interest of this fascinating play for the
historian, or student, of today lies in the fact that it appeared
precisely when it did, at the moment when the dramatic forms
popular with the 'baroque' generation of 1630 were facing a
strong challenge in the shape of a new, regular tragedy.

Having been offered to its first spectators, and enthusias-
tically welcomed by them, as a tragicomedy, *Le Cid* was to
become the subject of a long drawn-out, and at times acri-
monious, controversy between Corneille and his critics.
Although some of the exchanges consist of little more than
trivial personal attacks, the 'Querelle du Cid' did also give an
airing to important issues, central to the debate between the
irregular and the regular forms. As a result, the controversy
almost certainly helped to accelerate the general acceptance
of the new kind of tragedy, and determined Corneille's own
choice of subject and manner from *Horace* onwards. Moreover, in the case of *Le Cid* itself, Corneille was to drop the
label 'tragicomédie' in favour of 'tragédie' from the 1648
edition onwards, and was to do his best in subsequent
comments on the play, and even by discreet textual changes,
retrospectively to accommodate his early masterpiece to the
new aesthetic.

Although the principal reason for our continued interest
in *Le Cid* may perhaps reside in those intrinsic features
which make it one of the outstanding dramatic works of the

seventeenth century, and which are hardly affected by the
textual changes introduced in successive editions published
between 1637 and 1682, I shall nevertheless begin by looking
at the play in the context in which it was created. Since it was
written in response to the specific stimuli of the 1630s, I
should have preferred to have been able to select the original
text as the basis of my study. Most modern editors have been
content to reproduce the definitive text of 1682, however;
and although the 1637 text was reprinted by Maurice Cauchie (S.T.F.M., Paris, 1946) and more recently by Peter
Nurse (Harrap, London, 1978; re-issued by Blackwell, Oxford, 1988), it is certain that the 1682 version will remain the
more generally available. Reference will normally be made,
therefore, to this version as presented in the Bordas edition
(edited by G. Griffe, Paris, 1962; reprinted 1980); and unless
otherwise indicated, line numbers will refer to the 1682 text.
For the most part, textual changes between the 1637 version
and subsequent editions serve a purely stylistic purpose; some
of the more interesting among these changes will be dealt
with in my commentary. There are two changes of more
substance, however: the opening scene of the original version
disappears from 1660 onwards, a structural alteration of some
significance; and at the end of the play, the changes made in
Chimène's last speech have an important bearing on the way
we interpret the denouement. In both cases, it seemed useful
to give the 1637 text in full, and these passages will be found
in an Appendix for the benefit of those readers working from
a modern reprint of the 1682 text which does not provide this
basic textual aid.

Italic numbers in brackets, followed where appropriate by
a page reference, refer to numbered items in the Bibliography
at the end of this volume.

1

'Le milieu' and 'le moment'

T H E beginnings of modern drama in France can be pin-
pointed with an unusual degree of precision. An edict of the
Parlement de Paris in 1548 put an end, in Paris at any rate,
to the performance of the traditional mystery plays, whose
popular mixture of the sacred and the profane, the edifying
and the indecent, increasingly offended both the aesthetic
taste of the educated and the religious susceptibilities of the
devout. And in 1549 the publication of Du Bellay's *Défense
et illustration de la langue française* produced a stirring call
for a literary tragedy based on known examples surviving
from the ancient world. The challenge was taken up by the
humanist playwrights of the second half of the century; and
poets like Jodelle, Garnier and Montchrétien produced tragedies not without literary merit. Renaissance tragedy is, however, with very few exceptions, static and elegiac, and in many
cases excessively bookish in character. It was during this
period that the distinctive form we associate with French
classical tragedy – five acts in alexandrine couplets, with
alternating masculine and feminine rhymes – was firmly established; but the earliest works in particular display too great a
fondness for declamatory soliloquies, and at the other extreme
an over-indulgence in the rigid dialogue pattern of stichomythia: that is, the regular alternation of single-line speeches.
Overt moralising is universal, and the generally sententious
tone betrays the dominant influence of the Latin tragic poet
Seneca. Critical opinion long differed on the nature of stage
performance (if any) of these plays; and although the consen-
sus of modern opinion seems to be that most of them were
performed, this was usually outside the professional theatre.
The second half of the sixteenth century, marked by the Wars

of Religion, showed a serious decline in the fortunes of the theatre in Paris, and although some tragedies were performed by travelling companies, they were more typically written for, and played to, the cultured audiences of the courts and the colleges; as for the manner of their performance, this probably approximated, *mutatis mutandis,* to a modern 'concert performance' of an opera rather than to a fully theatrical *mise en scène.*

The more settled reign of Henri IV brought a new period of theatrical activity in Paris, where the dramatist Alexandre Hardy became the first example of a 'poète à gages', employed by the Comédiens du Roi at the Hôtel de Bourgogne theatre. In contrast with that of the humanist poets, Hardy's contribution to the evolution of serious drama was based on a practical sense of the theatre, though his literary style was lacking in grace and harmony. It would be wrong to think of Hardy as a popular playwright of no culture: his tragedies in particular show a familiarity with themes from classical mythology and ancient history. But he was not committed to a single dramatic formula, and his tragicomedies mark the beginning of the popular vogue for this freer genre. Although both theory and practice show clearly enough that the notion of regular drama was not unknown in the early years of the seventeenth century, the dominant fashion during the first three decades was for drama of irregular construction, and for a kind of subject-matter, and a literary style, that suggests to us the manner of our own Elizabethan and Jacobean dramatists, or that of Calderón and other playwrights of the Spanish Golden Age, rather than the disciplined classical manner that was to win general acceptance in the Paris theatres such a short time later. Let us look briefly at a few examples of the baroque drama of this period.

(i) In Hardy's tragedy *Scédase, ou l'Hospitalité violée* (c. 1610), two young men are offered hospitality, in their host's absence, by the latter's two daughters; they repay this by raping the girls and killing them, throwing the bodies down a well. The published text seems to indicate that all this takes place on stage.

(ii) In a tragicomedy by Hardy, *La Force du sang* (c. 1620), Acts I and II and the first part of Act III consist of events which take place seven years before the rest of the play. The heroine, out walking with her parents, is snatched away by the licentious son of the ruler: he rapes her while she is unconscious, and then sets her free. Seven years later, the child born to her of this encounter is accidentally injured at a tournament, and she and the boy are taken to the royal palace. She recognises the room in which she had been raped; the Prince, now older and wiser, repents of his crime, and the play ends with her marriage.

(iii) Théophile de Viau's tragedy *Pyrame et Thisbé* (1622) presents the same story (from Ovid) as is used by Shakespeare for the play within the play in *A Midsummer Night's Dream*. To circumvent their parents' enmity, the two lovers make a rendezvous outside the city walls. Thisbé arrives first, is frightened by a lion, and flees, dropping her cloak. Pyrame, finding the bloodstained garment, assumes she is dead and kills himself; Thisbé returns, discovers her lover's body, and kills herself in her turn. Both lovers, before dying, express their grief in long soliloquies. Thisbé's (of 118 lines) is best known for the couplet she addresses to the dagger stained with Pyrame's blood:

> Ha! voici le poignard qui du sang de son maître
> S'est souillé lâchement: il en rougit, le traître! (1227-28)

– lines which Boileau was later to criticise on grounds of poor taste. Pyrame's soliloquy takes 170 lines, of which no fewer than thirty are devoted to a single extended conceit:

> En toi, lion, mon âme a fait ses funérailles,
> Qui digères déjà mon cœur en tes entrailles.
> Reviens et me fais voir au moins mon ennemi.
> Encore tu ne m'as dévoré qu'à demi:
> Achève ton repas; tu seras moins funeste,
> Si tu m'es plus cruel. Achève donc ce reste,
> Ote-moi le moyen de te jamais punir.
> Mais ma douleur te parle en vain de revenir:

Depuis que ce beau sang passe en ta nourriture,
Tes sens ont dépouillé leur cruelle nature;
Je crois que ton humeur change de qualité,
Et qu'elle a plus d'amour que de brutalité... (1043-54)

(iv) In Corneille's own second play, the tragicomedy
Clitandre (1632), Acts II, III and IV are taken up with two
separate ambushes by disappointed lovers, in the same part of
the same wood at the same time. One man tries to force his
attentions on the girl he loves, who, although disguised as a
man, has forgotten to remove her hairpin, which betrays her
identity. The climax of this episode comes when, to avoid his
importunities, she plunges the hairpin into his eye; and this
gives rise to the following conceit, as Pymante addresses the
pin he has just plucked out, and blames it for not recognising
that his eye was a mirror framing the image of his mistress:

Bourreau qui secondant son courage inhumain,
Au lieu d'orner son poil, déshonorez sa main,
Exécrable instrument de sa brutale rage,
Tu devais pour le moins respecter son image.
Ce portrait accompli d'un chef-d'œuvre des cieux
Imprimé dans mon cœur, exprimé dans mes yeux,
Quoi que te commandât son âme courroucée,
Devait être adoré de ta pointe émoussée;
Quelque secret instinct te devait figurer
Que se prendre à mon œil c'était le déchirer... (1207-16)

(v) Several of these baroque dramas make use of the
device of the play within a play. A notable example is
Corneille's *L'Illusion comique,* produced just before *Le Cid*
in 1636, in which there are *three* levels of illusion, i.e. part of
the action represents a play within a play within a play.
Commenting on the structure of this work, Corneille described it as an 'étrange monstre', and drew attention to its
contrasts of tone between the 'comic' and the 'tragic'.

Now all of these attributes: plot devices such as disguise
and ambush; violent physical action on stage (rape and
attempted rape; a heroine pursued by a lion; duels, murders
and suicides); coarse behaviour juxtaposed with serious scenes

of an elevated nature; untidy features of composition such
as a gap of several years between the two halves of a play;
the structural complexities of the play within a play; self-
indulgent literary embellishment by means of absurdly far-
fetched conceits; and, subsuming all these details, the sheer
theatricality that is characteristic of this whole baroque
period: this is surely what we associate with Shakespeare and
his contemporaries, and specific parallels with plays like *A
Midsummer Night's Dream, A Winter's Tale* and *Romeo and
Juliet* immediately come to mind. How is it, then, if identical
features are to be found at the same time in representative
examples of French drama, that they were so soon to be
rejected by prevailing fashion, in favour of a chastened,
refined, simplified conception of tragedy? Why, just at the
time of *Le Cid,* did the exuberance of the baroque drama give
way to a kind of play that is commonly thought of as
appealing to the mind rather than to the eye, and that a
recent critic has characterised by invoking its 'intellectua-
lisme invétéré'? The reasons for this can be considered under
three heads: social, literary and theatrical; and I propose to
examine each of these factors briefly in turn.

By *social* factors, I mean the nature of the audience for
whom a play was destined, its composition in terms of class
and sex; the relationship between the cultural history of a
period (specifically as reflected in the taste of theatre audiences) and its political and social history. In this area, much
is of necessity speculative. For instance, the effects of peace
and settled political conditions after half a century of civil
war are difficult to assess with any real precision; but it is
certain that there was a new desire for refinement, and that
the civilising, predominantly feminine, influence of the early
salons can be seen reflected in the literature of the time. The
pastoral novels and plays which enjoyed such a vogue in the
1620s provided a vehicle, despite their stylised conventions,
for the delicate analysis of the psychology of love; and the
impact of this on the tragicomedy of the period can be seen in
the various hybrid forms such as the 'tragicomédie pastorale'
which came into being. Theatregoing became more respect-
able as the century progressed; witness the passage that Cor-

neille inserted into *L'Illusion comique* contrasting the 1630s
with the beginning of the century from this point of view:

> ... à présent le théâtre
> Est en un point si haut qu'un chacun l'idolâtre,
> Et ce que votre temps voyait avec mépris
> Est aujourd'hui l'amour de tous les bons esprits,
> L'entretien de Paris, le souhait des provinces,
> Le divertissement le plus doux de nos princes,
> Les délices du peuple, et le plaisir des grands... (1781-87)

Although there is sure to have been an element of wishful
thinking here, what Corneille's Alcandre says is largely con-
firmed by modern research. John Lough, for instance, has
shown from his examination of letters, memoirs and other
documentary evidence that by the time of *Le Cid* audiences
contained a greater proportion both of women and of the
educated classes than had been the case a generation earlier
(*29*, pp. 46 ff.).

One aspect of the social history of this period which had a
decided effect on the evolution of taste concerns the role of
Richelieu. In his determination to consolidate the stability of
the monarchy by encouraging orthodoxy and conservatism in
every aspect of French life, the Cardinal did not overlook the
important contribution of literature. On the one hand, the
Académie Française was founded under his patronage in
1635; while at the same time, his specific interest in the
theatre, and his ambition to make his mark as a dramatic
author, led to the creation of the 'Compagnie des cinq
auteurs' (Corneille was one of these) who worked under his
orders. The fact that Richelieu favoured a certain kind of
play was naturally a not unimportant factor in the evolution
of dramatic genres in the 1630s, and at the time of the
'Querelle du Cid' he made a decisive intervention when he
referred the controversy to the critical judgement of the new
Academy.

If we turn to the *literary* factors, the tendency towards
refinement, simplicity and self-discipline can of course be
measured with greater precision. Here the role of Malherbe is

of outstanding importance: Malherbe who, though not a very
talented poet himself, exercised a remarkable influence on
his fellow-poets, and of whom Boileau was to write:

> Enfin Malherbe vint, et le premier en France
> Fit sentir dans les vers une juste cadence.[2]

On the other hand, a nineteenth-century historian was to put
it rather differently: 'Enfin Malherbe vint, et la poésie, le
voyant venir, s'en alla'; and it is true that the whole drift of
his reforms was inimical to poetic inspiration and to the sort
of baroque imagination we have illustrated above. However,
Malherbe's doctrine did have one very important positive
result in the domain of dramatic poetry. Substituting for the
images and conceits of the Pléiade and their baroque succes-
sors a kind of verse appealing to the intelligence and the
common-sense of the reader, he helped to make of the
alexandrine a first-class vehicle for rational debate, for analyt-
ical soliloquy, and for the vigorous opposition of points of
view: in a word, for the dialogue typical of the new tragedy,
as this genre was to develop at the hands of Corneille and
others from 1640 onwards.

Another 'éminence grise' of this period was Chapelain, a
founder member of the Academy and author of the major
contribution to the 'Querelle du Cid'. In various occasional
writings from 1630 onwards, Chapelain had advocated adher-
ence to the three Unities, and he is rightly considered one of
the chief architects of the doctrines of French classicism.
However, it is important to realise that the doctrinal rules
governing classical tragedy were not imposed on unwilling, or
rebellious, practitioners: the initiative was taken by playwrights themselves, and credit for the first deliberately regular drama goes to Jean Mairet, whose *tragicomédie pastorale
Silvanire* was performed in 1630, and published with a
prefatory treatise in 1631: the result, not of pressure from
all-powerful theorists but of the ambition of a young man of

---

[2] *Art poétique* (1674), Canto I, ll. 131-32.

letters, inspired by Italian examples and the encouragement of his patron, the duc de Montmorency.

The 1630s saw a remarkable ferment of dramatic production: an unprecedented wealth of literary talent was devoted to the theatre, with half-a-dozen young playwrights – Mairet, Corneille, Rotrou, Tristan, Scudéry, Du Ryer – all competing for the favour of the public. They were prepared to ring the changes on the various dramatic genres: comedy and tragedy, besides the more popular tragicomedy and pastoral; and all of them were to begin with quite eclectic in their approach to the rules. Only gradually, in this atmosphere of intense competition, did the formula of regular tragedy succeed in gaining pre-eminence, based on the three unities of time, place and action, and acknowledging obedience to the 'bienséances', or proprieties: those unwritten rules which were in the final analysis to prove more important than the Unities themselves, constituting as they did a fourth, equally rigid unity: that of tone.

There was little hint before *Le Cid* that one of these ambitious young playwrights would soon stand head and shoulders above the rest. Corneille had written eight previous plays: the vintage baroque tragicomedy *Clitandre*; five comedies in which he had progressively experimented with regularity of time and place; the regular tragedy *Médée*; and a play, *L'Illusion comique*, which is nowadays acknowledged to be a masterpiece of baroque theatricality. When he turned to *Le Cid*, this was still in the same spirit of experimentation; but although *Le Cid* can only be fully understood and appreciated as emerging from the context of the 1630s, it was soon to be recognised as producing the sort of watershed in the history of dramatic literature that obliges us to think in terms of 'plays before *Le Cid*' and 'plays after *Le Cid*'.

If finally we turn to consider the *theatrical* factors, the material conditions in which plays of the period were presented to a theatre audience, we can see that not only was the classical drama of the seventeenth century not the creation of theorists in some ivory tower, it was not even the spontaneous expression of a literary avant-garde in search of the recipe for success with the more cultured part of their au-

diences. For side by side with the literary developments we
have sketched from irregular to regular, there can be traced a
parallel evolution in *mise en scène,* from one system which
derived from the mediaeval theatre to another which, once
established, was to remain in force for well over two hundred
years. The evolution in theatrical technique complements the
thinking of the avant-garde theorists and playwrights; and the
emergence of a classical 'doctrine', if it was partly an attempt
to work out a theoretical basis for a formula which would
satisfy the rational needs of an educated audience, was also a
response to the changing practice of the *décorateur.* And once
again *Le Cid* can be seen to constitute the hinge between the
old and the new: between the multiple set, or *décor simultané,* and the single perspective set.

When the religious theatre of the Middle Ages went
indoors from the market-place, it had retained the *mise en
scène* of the open air performance. In other words the
'mansions', or compartments, needed for the various scenes
of a play were all displayed side by side, and were all in
permanent view. Such a décor was symbolic, not representational, and its function was suggestive: the actors emerged
from, or positioned themselves in front of, a particular
compartment – the garden of Eden, or the inn at Bethlehem,
as it might be – and the whole acting area was deemed to
represent that location for the duration of the scene, until
this was cancelled by a corresponding indication for the scene
which followed. The same convention was still in force at the
Hôtel de Bourgogne in the early years of the seventeenth
century. The *décor simultané* had been modified; the number
of compartments settled at about five: for instance a king's
palace stage centre, flanked by the residences of other characters, with out-of-town features such as a coast (for ship-
wrecks) or a wood (for ambushes) occupying downstage
positions on each side. Supplementary locations could be
added by the use of painted backcloths; and indoor compartments were sometimes concealed by a curtain until needed.
This remained a perfectly valid dramaturgical system, as long
as the convention was accepted by playwrights, *décorateurs*
and spectators; but in the 1630s various factors conspired to

bring it under attack. The sketch-book of Laurent Mahelot, *décorateur* to the Hôtel de Bourgogne, in which are preserved his designs for 47 plays in that theatre's repertory up to the mid 1630s, shows that in some cases there is already a tendency to 'compose' the various elements needed for a play into a coherent whole (see *28*). Here too the example of the Italians is important, for educated playgoers would be familiar with the single perspective sets adopted by Italian designers and available in the form of published engravings.[3] And among the more articulate, cultured spectators there was a growing importance attached to the rationalist criterion of common-sense: they wanted a stage set to provide a realistic *representation* of place, not a symbolic suggestion. And since theatres at this time had no proscenium arch, and therefore no front curtain that could be lowered to permit changes of scene between acts, the call for a single representational set acquired a strong psychological support – support which, while it complemented the theoretical demand for the unity of place, was essentially independent of this requirement, which derived in principle from the unity of time (if the action of a play is limited to twenty-four hours or less, then there must be a strict limit on the range of locations it can cover...).

Le Cid was not performed at the Hôtel de Bourgogne, but by the rival company under the actor Mondory. Having travelled in the provinces for some years, this company had settled in the capital in 1629, bringing with it Corneille's first play, *Mélite,* from Rouen. Corneille's other early plays were probably also performed by Mondory, whose outstanding success as an actor-manager (he took over as leader of the company in 1634) depended partly on his own acting talent, and partly on the quality of the plays submitted for performance by Corneille and others; in this respect, *Le Cid* was to break all records. After changing their quarters a few times, Mondory and his colleagues had moved in 1634 to a convert-

---

[3] For instance Serlio's well-known designs for 'the comic scene', 'the tragic scene' and 'the satiric scene', reproduced in e.g. A. M. Nagler, *A Source Book in Theatrical History* (1952), New York, Dover Books, 1959, pp. 75-76.

ed tennis-court in the Marais district, the theatre taking the name of 'le théâtre du Marais' by which it was henceforth to be known. The detailed history of the Marais theatre is not so well documented as that of the Hôtel de Bourgogne: in particular, there is nothing corresponding to the valuable record provided for the latter theatre by Mahelot's *Mémoire.* On the other hand, the dimensions of the theatre are known quite precisely – it shared with other early theatre buildings in Paris the long, narrow shape of the converted *jeu de paume* (see *22*) – and in the absence of any evidence to the contrary it is reasonable to assume that the *mise en scène* at the Marais corresponded in general terms to the kind of set recorded by Mahelot.

We can be certain, therefore, that *Le Cid* was written for production on a compartmented stage; though the number of separate compartments had by now been further reduced. It is also certain, however, that the lack of absolutely precise textual indications as to the location of some scenes – possibly aided by the designer having made the compartments less distinct from each other as a move towards a coherent, unified set, as well as by the actors' casualness in denoting place by their position vis à vis the relevant compartment – laid the play open to criticism from the less benevolent among its early spectators; we shall examine examples of this sort of criticism later.

There are no doubt many ways in which *Le Cid* helped to bring about the demise of the *décor simultané,* and hastened the general acceptance of the single set with a perspective backcloth; but as W. L. Wiley points out, in one important respect 'it was not the artistic but the financial success' of Corneille's play that had this result (*41,* p. 192). As at other seventeenth-century theatres, the body of the hall, the *parterre,* at the Marais contained no seats, and was occupied by a large, lively, at times turbulent, crowd of standing spectators: bourgeois, artisans, lackeys, soldiers, pages – the atmosphere of the *parterre* must have had something in common with that of today's Promenade Concerts at the Albert Hall (if not of the better-behaved football crowd on the terraces); while the noble and well-to-do spectators (including the ladies) occupied the *loges,* or boxes, running down each side of the long building, and the *amphithéâtre,* or raised seating, at the far end. For *Le Cid,* however, so great was the pressure on places that, as a temporary expedient, extra seating was provided at the sides of the stage for noble patrons who could not otherwise secure a seat; to quote Mondory:

> La foule a été si grande à nos portes, et notre lieu s'est trouvé si petit, que les recoins du théâtre qui servaient les autres fois comme de niches aux pages, ont été des places de faveur pour les cordons bleus, et la scène y a été d'ordinaire parée de croix de chevaliers de l'ordre du Saint-Esprit.[4]

This temporary expedient was to last over a hundred years. These highly-prized (and highly-priced) seats became such an important source of income that theatre companies could not afford to do away with them, and new theatres even incorporated stage seats as a permanent feature of their design. The presence of exhibitionist young noblemen on stage can hardly have been conducive to the realism of a single representational set; but more immediately, this feature helped to kill off the multiple stage: there was no future in a compartmented set, once spectators were seated between the acting area and the compartments to which it related.

Le Cid, then, was created in conditions of vigorous competition, at a time of rapidly changing attitudes to the new doctrines of regular drama: doctrines which, if Corneille's own attitude up to 1637 was still very open-minded, his play nevertheless helped decisively to establish. Let us now look at the play itself, in the context in which it was created; and let us start by considering Corneille's choice of subject for *Le Cid.*

---

[4] Letter of 18 January 1637 to Balzac.

2

The Subject

In his study of tragicomedy, H. C. Lancaster lists five criteria distinguishing this genre from that of tragedy:

(i)   The structure is that of the *drame libre,* by which the story is dramatised from its beginnings without regard for any dramatic unity except that of interest.

(ii)   The events treated are serious, secular, non-historic, and *romanesque.*

(iii)   The denouement is happy.

(iv)   The leading personages are aristocratic, but bourgeois and plebeians may be introduced in subordinate roles. The shepherd of the pastoral is excluded.

(v)   The addition of comic passages, though frequent, is not an essential characteristic.[5]

The second and third of these criteria are closely related, involving as they do the choice of subject and the most important aspect of its treatment.

French tragedy, in the eighty-odd years since Jodelle had inaugurated the genre, had with very few exceptions taken its subjects from one of three sources: the Bible, ancient history or mythology. Even the few isolated examples of tragedy on a modern historical subject (such as Montchrétien's *L'Écossaise* of 1601, which deals with Mary Queen of Scots) had exemplified in their way the feature that was regarded as absolutely essential for tragedy, namely the guarantee of historical truth. If the use of the epithet 'historical' may seem surprising to a more sceptical generation of students, we

[5] *The French Tragicomedy: its origin and development from 1552 to 1628,* Baltimore, Furst, 1907, p. xxiv.

should remember that the authority of the biblical texts remained virtually unchallenged at this date, and that the corpus of classical legends had acquired a similar authority by virtue of the antiquity of their sources.

Tragicomedy, by contrast, was essentially a *romanesque,* or fictional, genre. Its subjects were characteristically taken from mediaeval or Renaissance romance (for instance, the plot of an early, and very successful, tragicomedy, Garnier's *Bradamante* of 1582, comes from the *Orlando Furioso*); or from later Italian short stories or Spanish novels (*Don Quixote* was to prove a fertile source); alternatively, the subject-matter was invented, but conformed to the sort of plot-material that spectators would be accustomed to find in contemporary novels. Thus Corneille's *Clitandre,* the subject of which is wholly of the playwright's own invention, exemplifies the popular 'chain of lovers' (Clitandre loves Caliste, who loves and is loved by Rosidor, who is loved by Dorise, who is loved by Pymante). The jealousy of unrequited love, on the part of Dorise and Pymante, produces the details of the plot (disguise, ambush, etc.); but since this is tragicomedy, not comedy, some of the characters are sufficiently high-born for affairs of state to be involved: Clitandre and Rosidor are the favourites, respectively, of the ruler and the crown prince of Scotland, where (for no apparent reason) this bizarre piece is set. Rosidor is nearly assassinated; and Clitandre, wrongly suspected of treason, is sentenced to death. All is cleared up, however, in time for the happy ending in which not only Rosidor and Caliste are united, but also (in the interests of symmetry) Clitandre and Dorise, even though they have shown no interest in each other throughout the play. The luckless Pymante, who has already lost an eye, is also punished by being left without a partner.

Such a tissue of romanesque contrivance, filled out by the plot details, and embellished by the literary conceits, illustrated above (p. 15), must seem a far remove from *Le Cid,* where the stirring heroics, and the tender expression of frustrated love, are set in the framework, not of cloak-and-dagger intrigue in some non-existent Ruritania, but of a well-known episode in the authentic historical conflict between Spain and the Moorish invaders. Is it merely a question of the difference between a mediocre play, written by an inexperienced playwright according to a mechanical formula, and a masterpiece in which the same playwright, now in full possession of his creative powers, made the most of the possibilities offered by the well-established popular genre? Or should we rather look for another label for a work which so transcends the limitations hitherto displayed by this romanesque type of play?

As has been said, the basic subject of *Le Cid* belongs to the domain of fact, not fiction; but by the time it reached Corneille's hands, the story of the eleventh-century Rodrigo de Bivar had undergone such a substantial modification in the epics and popular ballads of the following centuries that the unscrupulous, opportunist adventurer of historical fact had been transformed into a legendary representative of the chivalric ideal. The young chieftain's prowess in battle against the Moors is authenticated, and the account of his marriage to Ximena also appears in fairly early texts; but whereas the first stages of the legend add the significant detail that his bride is the daughter of a man he had killed in a duel, in these earliest sources it is a marriage demanded by Ximena, and granted by the King, as an act of reparation towards a noble family Rodrigo has deprived of its head. Once this judicial transaction had been transmuted by the imagination of a later poet into the consummation of a love existing before the duel – with the father's death no longer constituting the reason for the marriage, but acting as an obstacle to it – the dramatic potential of the legend was considerable; and it was a Spanish playwright, Guillén de Castro, who took the decisive step and made a play on the subject, *Las Mocedades del Cid* (*The Youthful Exploits of the Cid*), which was performed in Valencia in 1618 and published in 1621.[6]

Castro's play, which provided Corneille with his principal source, typified in its free, episodic structure the Spanish *comedia* of its day, and would certainly have satisfied the

---

[6] See the edition by Victor Said Armesto, Madrid, Espasa-Calpe, 1962.

criteria for the irregular French tragicomedy of the 1620s and early 1630s. Its action takes place over three years; it occupies eight different locations, with each act presenting a succession of disconnected scenes; and the play has an unambiguously happy ending, when the marriage between Rodrigo and Ximena is arranged to take place immediately. As regards its romanesque quality, Castro takes over from the legends a number of subsidiary episodes: in Act I, for instance, Diego, publicly insulted by Ximena's father, tests each of his three sons in turn before engaging Rodrigo to defend the family honour; and in Act III Rodrigo gives assistance to a leper, then falls into a mystic sleep in which the leper, transformed into Saint Lazarus, pronounces his blessing on the young man's enterprise. Generally speaking, the Spanish play is a good deal more spectacular and theatrical than Corneille's, with more action shown on stage.

But although Corneille has pruned the Spanish plot of certain self-contained episodes, and although he has managed to accommodate the subject to the unities of time and place, it is still unmistakably the same subject, and the details of the action that Corneille does preserve are taken over virtually unchanged. Rodrigue, the untried young knight, is loved by the Infante, as well as by Chimène, whose love he returns. After the quarrel between the two fathers, he champions his family honour and challenges Chimène's father, the experienced general Don Gomès, whom he kills. Chimène in her turn takes up her father's cause, calling on the King for vengeance on his killer. Before the case can be decided, Rodrigue defeats the Moorish invaders in a night battle, becoming the saviour of his country and earning the title of 'Cid'. Don Sanche, who comes forward as Chimène's champion, is allowed to represent her in single combat; and when he in his turn has been defeated by Rodrigue, the King's judgement is pronounced: Chimène is ordered to marry Rodrigue after a year's delay. Apart from the change in the time-scale, Corneille is faithful to his source as regards the characters, as well as the details of plot that he takes over. The Infanta is unchanged, and the alteration of Chimène's champion (an Aragonese giant in Castro's play) into Don Sanche is of minor importance. As for the hero and heroine, their motivation and attitudes remain remarkably similar to those of their Spanish counterparts.

If the theme of love versus duty, of the union of two well-matched young lovers threatened by their allegiance to the aristocratic ethic they both profess, is what has always attracted spectators and readers to Corneille's masterpiece, this is no more than a development at his hands of something that was already present in the Spanish play. Indeed, before being adapted to the heroic ethic that Corneille recognised in the French nobility of his own generation, the mediaeval legend had been acclimatised in the Spain of the early seventeenth century, where the *pundonor* (a punctilious concern with personal and family honour) provided one of the predominant themes of Golden Age drama.

Whether this is to be regarded as a potentially tragic theme, or one more appropriate to the romanesque genres of the Spanish *comedia* and the French heroic tragicomedy, will no doubt largely depend on the subjective views each of us holds on the nature of tragedy. I shall of course attempt to analyse the emotional impact of the play when I come to examine in detail the way in which Corneille has handled his theme; but the following remarks are perhaps not inappropriate at this preliminary stage. Compared with the subjects chosen by Corneille himself for his tragedies from 1640 onwards, and by Racine and other authors of tragedies later in the century, the subject of *Le Cid* is lacking both in the high seriousness and in the sense of the inevitable that we look for in all great tragedy; and as Helen Gardner has observed, 'tragedy that is not "great" is not tragedy, but "failed tragedy"'.[7] Corneille's story is after all one of private relationships, even if these are set against a background of affairs of state; moreover, the obstacle to the happiness of Rodrigue and Chimène is the product of pure chance: a quarrel between their fathers that might never have taken place. It is not even a case of a long-standing feud, as in

[7] *Religion and Literature,* London, Faber and Faber, 1981, p. 17.

Romeo and Juliet or *Pyrame et Thisbé;* though in both of these examples – plays with a 'tragic' outcome, but whose subjects derive from the stock of romanesque material that furnished the tragicomedy of the period – the difference bet-ween happy and unhappy ending depends entirely on a chance sequence of events. Not so in true tragedy: there is all the difference in the world between gratuitous chance and genuine tragic fate, and we may contrast the romanesque inconsequentiality of these examples of the 'pères ennemis' theme with the tragic inevitability possessed by that of the 'frères ennemis' that was to be chosen by Racine for his first play, where the fratricidal hatred innate in the blood of the protagonists – the warring sons of Oedipus – is so powerful that it can be satisfied only in their mutual destruction. Other playwrights writing serious drama in the 1630s had acknowl-edged that one way in which tragedy was to be distinguished from tragicomedy was by the seriousness and the inevitability of its subject-matter: Mairet's *Sophonisbe* (1634) had recog-nised these qualities in the Carthaginian heroine's hopeless fight against the power of Rome, Rotrou's *Hercule mourant* (1635) in the fated death of a mythological hero. Corneille himself, in *Médée* (1636), had chosen one of the great mythological subjects of antiquity, illustrated by Euripides and Seneca; and we may be sure that when he wrote *Le Cid,* he was quite deliberately making a different sort of choice, and consciously reverting to the more popular subject-matter of tragicomedy.

It is not only modern scholars, motivated by a historical approach and aided by a historian's hindsight, who attach such importance to this question of the genesis of *Le Cid,* and of the genre to which it belongs. In Corneille's own day there was a vigorous debate, among both the *doctes,* or academic theorists of the literary scene, and the playwrights themselves, about the relationship between the new regular dramatic forms and certain kinds of subject-matter; indeed, this can be seen to have constituted the central issue of the 'Querelle du Cid', however diffuse and confused some of the argument may have been. On the other hand, we may assume that the overwhelming success of *Le Cid* with its first audiences in

1636-37 was due to essential qualities that the theatregoing public at large did not consciously relate to this theoretical debate. As a contemporary wrote, looking back on the play's initial impact:

> Il est malaisé de s'imaginer avec quelle approbation cette pièce fut reçue de la Cour et du public. On ne se pouvait lasser de la voir, on n'entendait autre chose dans les compagnies, chacun en savait quelque partie par cœur, on la faisait apprendre aux enfants, et en plusieurs endroits de la France il était passé en proverbe de dire: *Cela est beau comme le Cid.*[8]

Let us now attempt to assess the qualities which so impressed the play's first spectators.

---

[8] See Pellisson, *Relation contenant l'histoire de l'Académie Française* (1653), in *31*, p. 57.

3

'Beau comme *Le Cid*'

IF we make a point of trying to approach *Le Cid* from the point of view of its first spectators, rather than from that of a modern reader, there are certain conventions that we must take into account. To begin with, there are the staging conditions described above (p. 20). To quote the author himself, in his *Examen* (1660) to the play:

> Tout s'y passe donc dans Séville, et garde ainsi quelque espèce d'unité de lieu en général; mais le lieu particulier change de scène en scène, et tantôt c'est le palais du Roi, tantôt l'appartement de l'Infante, tantôt la maison de Chimène, et tantôt une rue ou place publique.

By the time he came to write these words, Corneille was very critical of the former practice of a *mise en scène* based on the multiple set, for he confesses in the *Discours des trois unités,* published in the same year, that 'sans doute il y a quelque excès dans cette licence'; nevertheless, his text provides valuable first-hand confirmation of how that practice had worked out in this specific instance. *Le Cid* had, according to its author, required four locations: the King's council-chamber, which we may imagine to have been upstage centre; flanking it on either side, the Infanta's room in the royal palace and Chimène's house; and in between and in front of these indoor locations, the open street. My commentary on the text will bear this convention in mind, and I shall indicate any difficulties of interpretation that it may appear to produce. For the time being, let us merely note the playwright's own comment: 'On détermine aisément [le lieu particulier] pour les scènes détachées; mais pour celles qui ont leur liaison

ensemble, comme les quatre dernières du premier acte, il est
malaisé d'en choisir un qui convienne à toutes' (*Examen*).

The second consideration concerns the acting conventions
of the time: less tangible, but equally essential to a proper
appreciation of the way in which the play must have been
received in 1637. Mondory, who played Rodrigue, had made
his name in a variety of roles, but it was a play produced
shortly before *Le Cid* which had provided him with the part
in which he gave his outstanding performance, to which there
are abundant contemporary tributes. This was a tragedy, *La
Mariane,* by Tristan l'Hermite, in which Mondory played the
violent, passionate Herod, whose jealousy drives him to kill
the wife, Mariamne, whom he loves. Mondory's portrayal of
a wide range of emotions – the Jewish King's jealous fury, his
desire for vengeance, his remorse after his wife's death, and
his final attack of madness – constituted such a physical *tour
de force* that when Tristan's play was revived in August 1637
the actor suffered an apoplectic fit on stage which brought his
professional career to a sudden end. This anecdote suggests a
violent declamatory manner in which the rhetorical portrayal
of stylised passions takes precedence over coherence of char-
acterisation; and although seventeenth-century spectators
were to pay tribute to the naturalness and human appeal of
his characters – as Boileau was to write, 'Tout Paris pour
Chimène a les yeux de Rodrigue'[9] – such comments must
necessarily be interpreted in a contemporary context. If much
less violent than Tristan's tragedy in the range of passions it
depicts, *Le Cid* was nevertheless written, *mutatis mutandis,*
in the rhetorical manner of the day for spectators who wanted
to be moved, excited or exalted by a combination of the
poet's craft and the actor's talent.

A c t   I

The play had opened, in the original text of 1637, with a
short scene of 32 lines between Elvire and Chimène's father,

---

[9] *Satire* IX (1668), l. 232.

which was suppressed in the definitive version of the play, while the original I, ii was expanded to make a longer opening scene between Chimène and her *confidente*. [10] In both versions, the tone of the introductory scene(s) is that of comedy: the subject under discussion, as well as the flavour of the dialogue, are reminiscent of the group of comedies from *Mélite* (1629) to *La Place Royale* (1634), whose style Corneille was later to characterise collectively as 'une peinture de la conversation des honnêtes gens'. [11]

The closing lines of the original opening scene, as Le Comte leaves for the council-chamber:

> Le Roi doit à son fils choisir un gouverneur,
> Ou plutôt m'élever à ce haut rang d'honneur;
> Ce que pour lui mon bras chaque jour exécute
> Me défend de penser qu'aucun me le dispute

do, it is true, contain a hint of the dramatic conflict that is to develop, though the point is not elaborated. Similarly, the heroine's cautious 'dans ce grand bonheur je crains un grand revers' is no more than an evocation of the conventional 'wheel of fortune' image, and there is no reason at this stage to anticipate the particular nature, or the gravity, of the 'revers' that will shortly threaten the lovers' happiness. For the rest, the relationship between the heroine and her *confidente,* her curiosity about her father's opinion of Rodrigue, and Elvire's account of the conversation with Le Comte, all suggest the genteel discourse of literary comedy.

It is not easy to guess why Corneille should have run these two scenes together, especially since the 52 lines of the original have been expanded to 58 lines in the later version. The new version draws heavily on the original text, and the conversation now reported by Elvire is in fact that which had taken place between Le Comte and herself in the 1637 version; it will be noted that lines 25-38 are a faithful transcript of

[10] For the 1637 text of the opening scenes, see Appendix.
[11] *Examen* (1660) to *Mélite*.

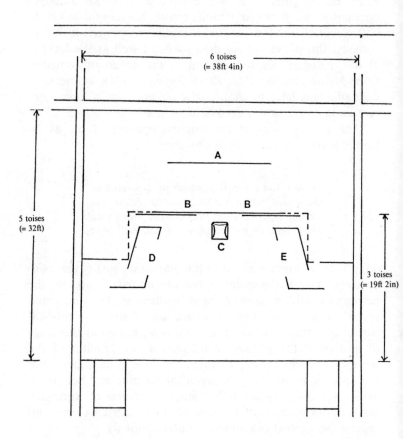

Fig. (i) Ground-plan of the stage of the Théâtre du Marais, with an indication of the possible décor for the first performances of *Le Cid* in 1636-37 (A: palace backcloth; B: palace with arch; C: throne; D: Chimène's house; E: the Infante's apartments).

Fig. (ii)   Axonometric drawing to accompany ground-plan in Fig. (i). Courtesy of Dr J. Golder, University of New South Wales.

that conversation, and similarly the last ten lines of scene i
(1682) closely resemble the ten closing lines of I, ii (1637).

The introduction of the Infante in the next scene (which
brings into play the compartment on the opposite side of the
stage, facing Chimène's house), surely suggests that this character – the excluded third party in a triangular love-rela-
tionship – is likely to constitute the obstacle to the happiness
of Chimène and Rodrigue. It is true that this scene for
the first time introduces the notions of *la générosité* and *la
gloire,* features of the aristocratic ethic that certainly lift the
level of the dialogue above that of 'la conversation des
honnêtes gens'; but even so, it hardly differs from that of a
play like *Don Sanche d'Aragon* (1649), that Corneille was to
label a 'comédie héroïque'. It is the Infante who formulates
the first *sentences,* or moral maxims, of the play: a characteristic feature of the more elevated heroic style; [12] but if the first
of these: 'L'amour est un tyran qui n'épargne personne' (81)
suggests that the Princess herself may be forced to threaten
the happy outcome of the lovers' relationship, and the second: 'dans les belles âmes / Le seul mérite a droit de
produire des flammes' (93-94) shows her awareness of an
excuse she could fall back on for such conduct, the further
development of the scene reassures us that she has the
will-power to resist this temptation:

> Quand je vis que mon cœur ne se pouvait défendre,
> Moi-même je donnai ce que je n'osais prendre.
> Je mis, au lieu de moi, Chimène en ses liens,
> Et j'allumai leurs feux pour éteindre les miens.   (101-04)

Indeed, by the end of scene ii, it seems that the Infante has
revealed herself as a passive character, who is determined not
to intervene as a threat to the happiness of Rodrigue and
Chimène, and whose resignation is characterised by these
paradoxical expressions of her plight:

[12] For a study of the *sentence* in Corneille, see *40*; and in seventeenth-
century drama more generally, *39* pp. 316-33.

> Je travaille à le perdre, et le perds à regret   (115)

> Ma plus douce espérance est de perdre l'espoir   (135)

Generally speaking, the function of the opening scenes may be said to be to establish the heroic tone of the play: that of the early comedies, suitably heightened by the rank of the characters and the vocabulary in which they express their hopes and their fears. The fortunes of the love between Rodrigue and Chimène are clearly going to be the subject of the play, but so far there is no indication of the source, or the seriousness, of the obstacle to that love.

Scene iii provides the first of the 'street scenes', as the two fathers come out from the palace where the council has met, and immediately give expression to their disagreement. At first the quarrel is one-sided, as Don Diègue responds in a conciliatory manner (161-64) to Le Comte's provocation, and attempts to bring the subject of discussion round to the prospective marriage of their offspring. But Le Comte's wounded self-esteem will not be appeased in this way, and he resorts to sarcasm (170ff.), taunting the older man with the fact that he is no longer capable of instructing the young Prince by example (183-84). Don Diègue's reply is a dignified reminder of his past exploits, but this goads Le Comte into a petulant display of arrogance. In this speech (191ff.) the expression of his *gloire* is reduced to crude self-advertisement, and there is even a reminder of the braggart Matamore of *L'Illusion comique* in his use of hyperbole:

> Et qu'a fait après tout ce grand nombre d'années
> Que ne puisse égaler une de mes journées?

Like Matamore, Le Comte endows his sword with his own soldierly virtue, and in another bombastic example of synecdoche he equates his very name with his heroic achievements:

> Grenade et l'Aragon tremblent quand ce fer brille;
> Mon nom sert de rempart à toute la Castille.

Don Diègue's next speech (207ff.), though it contains a generous appreciation of the Count's merits:

> Quand l'âge dans mes nerfs a fait couler la glace,
> Votre rare valeur a bien rempli ma place

is hardly calculated to placate his rival; and the conclusion to this speech, which we can read as a move to break off the argument:

> Vous voyez toutefois qu'en cette concurrence
> Un monarque entre nous met quelque différence

has the opposite effect, of bringing it to a violent climax.

Like all passages of stichomythia, if this device is handled with discretion,[13] lines 215ff. convey admirably the rise in the emotional temperature. The fact that Don Diègue speaks the second line in each couplet gives him the dialectical, and therefore the psychological, advantage. Each time, up to line 224, his *réplique,* reinforced by the expected rhyme, 'caps' what his rival has just said; and the cumulative effect is of a mounting tension that must be broken by the frustrated Don Gomès. When this occurs, the Comte temporarily takes the initiative, the broken line 225 allowing him to deliver both rhymes in the couplet that culminates in the celebrated *soufflet*; it should be noted, too, that Chimène's father is the first to use *tutoiement,* indicating the abandonment of all formal restraint. The brisk action continues to line 230, as Diègue attempts to draw his sword to avenge the affront, and has to confess that he lacks the strength to wield it. The scene ends, in the original edition, with ten lines in which the Comte exults in his rival's shame; though it is worth noting that the last four lines disappear in the 1682 text – no doubt because the final couplet:

---

[13] But cf. a much cruder use in Corneille's *La Suivante* (1634), where a whole scene of forty lines (III, ii) is composed of single-line *répliques* exchanged by two characters.

> Tu dédaignes ma vie!
> > – En arrêter le cours
> Ne serait que hâter la Parque de trois jours

with its explicit reference to the finite passage of time, lowers the tone too obviously from lofty heroics to a verbal play more fit for comedy.

This lively, dramatic scene is followed by a static soliloquy: an excellent example of virtuoso rhetoric whose success is attested; not least by Corneille's own mock-heroic parody in *Le Menteur* (1643):

> O vieillesse facile! ô jeunesse impudente!
> O de mes cheveux gris honte trop évidente!...   (V, ii)

In the original passage ('O rage, ô désespoir! ô vieillesse ennemie!...') we find the standard rhetorical features of apostrophe (237, 245-46, 247-48, 257ff.), anaphora (241-42) and antithesis (250). Imagery of a conventional kind is prominent (*blanchir,* 239; *flétrir... lauriers,* 240; *précipice,* 248; *glace,* 256); thematically significant words are placed at the rhyme with obvious effect (*ennemie - infamie*; *guerriers - lauriers*; *bonheur - honneur*; *offense - défense*); and the diction is further maintained at a lofty level by the relationship between the metrical unit of the alexandrine couplet and the grammatical unit of the sentence. The end-stopped lines which predominate are varied by couplets with a distinctive structure, in which the two lines are linked by a mild *enjambement*: the import of the full line may be repeated in condensed form in the half-line *rejet,* while the opposing half-line conveys a sharply contrasting meaning:

> Faut-il de votre éclat voir triompher le Comte
> Et mourir sans vengeance, // ou vivre dans la honte?

In its original form, the soliloquy concluded with two further examples of this same feature. In the first, the meaning expressed by the *rejet* is amplified in that of the full line which follows:

> Si Rodrigue est mon fils, // il faut que l'amour cède
> Et qu'une ardeur plus haute à ses flammes succède;

while in the second, the continuous line and a half is
devoted to the amplification of the sense of the first half-line

> Mon honneur est le sien, // et le mortel affront
> Qui tombe sur mon chef rejaillit sur son front.

All experienced students of Corneille will recognise this
structure, which gives eloquent reinforcement to a simple
idea, as typical of the playwright's handling of the alexandrine couplet;[14] and the two instances cited from the end of
the speech in the 1637 text had brought the soliloquy to a
dignified conclusion, at the same time forecasting the theme
of the encounter between father and son.

Scene v introduces the hero, Don Rodrigue, as an impet-
uous, warm-blooded youth. His impulsive reply to his father's challenge (261-62) and his impatience with Don Diègue's
prosy, sententious manner (266-67, 275-81) lead to the climax (283), at which his shattered self-confidence finds expression in a single monosyllable, while his father continues
to utter conventional moral truths in dogmatic maxims (284,
285). The scene comes to a striking close with a couplet in
which a slow, elegiac line and a half are juxtaposed with an
energetic half-line containing four monosyllabic imperatives.

Act I scene vi must in its time have been one of the most
celebrated scenes in the whole repertory of serious French
drama. So-called 'stances lyriques' had been introduced some
years earlier, and had rapidly established themselves in popular favour as a means of drawing attention to a mono-
logue delivered at a point of emotional tension or moral
decision (see *24*; *39,* pp. 285ff.). Twenty years later, this
feature of baroque dramaturgy was to fall foul of the rationalistic critique of d'Aubignac, who maintained that it was not

---

[14] The use of the same structure by Racine is noted in R. A. Sayce,
'Racine's Style: Periphrasis and Direct Statement', *The French Mind: Studies
in honour of Gustave Rudler,* Oxford, Clarendon Press, 1952, pp. 70-89.

appropriate to the spontaneous expression of emotion because, if the alexandrine was to be accepted as the conventional counterpart of real-life speech, then the complex, artificial forms of the 'stances' must represent a poetic composition, and 'il faut que l'acteur qui les récite ait eu quelque temps suffisant pour y travailler, ou pour y faire travailler' (*9*, p. 263). By 1660, the date of the *Examens,* Corneille was finding it difficult to justify his practice in his earlier plays; and although he dissented from d'Aubignac's general censure, he went so far as to admit that 'il faut éviter le trop d'affectation', and continued in a spirit not dissimilar to the abbé's:

> C'est par là que les stances du *Cid* sont inexcusables et les mots de *peine* et *Chimène,* qui font la dernière rime de chaque strophe, marquent un jeu du côté du poète, qui n'a rien de naturel du côté de l'acteur (*Examen d'Andromède*).

In 1636-37, however, such metrical virtuosity was much to the theatregoing public's taste; and it may be noted that far from attenuating the 'affectation' of the original in the post-1637 editions, Corneille in fact emphasised it by introducing further examples of antithesis (313, 314), apostrophe (318) and anaphora (323-24).

In an important sense, the epithet 'lyrique' is a misnomer. From a technical point of view, Rodrigue's *stances* may show the requisite metrical patterns; but they do not suggest a spontaneous expression of emotion. All is carefully controlled, and an examination of the way in which the speaker analyses, and resolves, his dilemma reveals a dialectical structure as rigorous as that which typifies the soliloquies of Corneille's later plays. The decorative imagery of the opening stanza (*percé, atteinte... mortelle, coup qui me tue*) should not mislead us: even Rodrigue's affective reactions (*Misérable vengeur... Et malheureux objet*, 293-94) are recorded in the form of a balanced antithesis; and lines 299-300 express a simple intellectual assessment of the dilemma, even if the rhyme *peine - Chimène,* reinforced by the adjective *étrange* in the affective position, undoubtedly supplies emotional overtones. Stanza 2 presents a static reiteration of the dilem-

ma, calling on various rhetorical devices to emphasise the
opposition of *honneur* and *amour* (302): in lines 303-04 these
dominant ideas are forcefully contrasted by the repeated
juxtaposition of the same parts of speech; in 305-06 the *triste
choix* is spelt out by grammatically similar formulas (*trahir
ma flamme... vivre en infâme*) linked by the rhyme; and the
insistent rhyme *peine - Chimène* reinforces the pair of rhetorical questions in 309-10. Antitheses abound in stanza 3,
reaching their most condensed form in the doubly contrasting
pair of apostrophes in line 311, and in the following line with
its contrasting pair of epithets (*noble et dure*) and the powerful oxymoron *aimable tyrannie*. The concepts are juxtaposed yet again at the rhyme, first in the abstract epithets
généreuse - amoureuse and then in the linked pair of nouns
bonheur - honneur; and once more the affective quality of the
rhyme *peine - Chimène* is outweighed by the rhetorical analysis of lines 319-20 with their striking anaphora.

Stanza 4 offers a false resolution of the dilemma; and it
seems certain that the antithetical presentation of alternatives
(323-24) is strengthened in the variants of the later editions:
Chimène will 'hate' Rodrigue if he avenges his father, but will
'despise' him if he does not. However, the temptation to
suicide as a way out (329-30) is immediately rejected in
Stanza 5 in the neat conceit of *un trépas si mortel à ma
gloire*. And in the final stanza, the positive resolution takes
the place of the false one. The antithesis *père-maîtresse* is no
longer (as in 303, 311, 322) presented as an equation: instead,
one term is given clear priority over the other. The refrain
now takes on a somewhat facile connotation: *Ne soyons plus
en peine... Si l'offenseur est père de Chimène* hardly does
justice to the depth of sentiment implied in line 343. On the
other hand, line 344 ('Je rendrai mon sang pur comme je l'ai
reçu') crystallises in poetic form Rodrigue's chivalrous resolve: here is a line capable, with its felicitous juxtaposition
of the literal and the figurative, of carrying an emotional
charge that is lacking from much of this scene.

It is a scene which presents real problems for the modern
student – and in a different way, no doubt, for the director
and actor in the theatre. Might one suggest that a possible

way to come to terms with such a virtuoso set-piece, whose metrical form, with its stylised rhythms, repetitions and antithetical patterns, clearly does put it in a different category from the soliloquies of established classical tragedy which share that genre's overall pursuit of psychological coherence, is to regard it as the equivalent of the operatic aria? As in an opera by Monteverdi, baroque tragicomedy similarly used the 'story-line' to create opportunities for static 'arias', 'duets' or 'recitatives' in which the dramatist could rise to the challenge and display the range of his poetic craftsmanship.

A C T   I I

The opening scene of this act – another street-scene, presumably – presents Chimène's father in unrepentant mood, accompanied by a minor character whose role, although he is a 'gentilhomme castillan', is little more than that of a *confident*. The conversation is sententious in tone, with several examples of the maxim (369-70, 372) or the near-maxim, similar in its epigrammatic form, but less detached from its context (366, 376, 387). The dialogue gains in urgency from 383 onwards, with lines split round the caesura (384, 391) and a brief fragment of stichomythia; and in a four-line coda to the scene the Comte reasserts the principle of the *pundonor* that is the criterion of his whole conduct.

As well as illustrating this typically Spanish motif for the knowledgeable spectator, such passages would of course also have a powerful topical reference. Micheline Sakharoff writes that 'le Comte et Don Diègue deviennent les symboles de deux morales contradictoires, celle toute féodale qu'exprime le Comte avec insolence, se faisant ainsi le représentant d'une noblesse frondeuse et insoumise, opposée au joug d'un souverain absolu; l'autre, plus en accord avec la politique de Richelieu, exprimée par Don Diègue qui réussit à intégrer la vieille notion d'honneur dans l'ordre présent et, sans renoncer à la gloire, le met cependant au service du roi' (*38*, pp. 118-19). For H. C. Lancaster, similarly, Don Gomès 'rep-

resents the turbulent princes of Corneille's day, and his down-
fall is a forerunner of theirs' (*27,* Part II, I, p. 124).

It should be noted in passing that in revising his text for
the 1682 edition, Corneille chose to round this scene off with
a resounding 'thematic' rhyme – a further example of the
rhyme *bonheur* – *honneur* to add to those already contained
in the 1637 text[15] – and with a couplet which possesses a
quite remarkable degree of phonetic identity over the whole
two lines:

> Et l'*on p*eut *me ré*dui*re à vivre sans* b*onheur,*
> Mais n*on p*as *me ré*soud*re à vivre sans honneur.*

The effect of such a 'super-rich' rhyme, combined with this
degree of 'isometry' between the two lines,[16] may perhaps be
compared with that of the rhyming couplet with which
Shakespeare often decisively concludes a blank verse passage.

Rodrigue's arrival in scene ii starts with a brisk confrontation. The Comte, at first incredulous at the young man's
audacity, moves on to acknowledgement of his valour and of
the chivalric qualities that make him such a desirable match
for his daughter; and having failed to dissuade Rodrigue from
the duel, finally accepts his challenge. Whatever Corneille's
spectators may have been meant to think of Le Comte's
behaviour in the previous scene, his manner here is one of
simple dignity; it is striking that Rodrigue's maxim 'A qui
venge son père, il n'est rien impossible' finds something like
an echo in Le Comte's final couplet:

> Viens, tu fais ton devoir, et le fils dégénère
> Qui survit un moment à l'honneur de son père.

---

[15] The original text had contained three instances of *honneur* rhyming
with *bonheur,* and seven other cases in which *honneur* appeared at the
rhyme.

[16] The term is used by J. G. Cahen, *Le Vocabulaire de Racine,* Paris,
Droz, 1946, p, 166.

The whole scene is animated by what Nadal and other modern interpreters have taught us to refer to as 'l'éthique de la gloire' (see *32, 33*); and while lines such as 409-10:

> Mes pareils à deux fois ne se font point connaître
> Et pour leurs coups d'essai veulent des coups de maître

or 411-12:

> ... tout autre que moi
> Au seul bruit de ton nom pourrait trembler d'effroi

may seem to us to express this spirit in somewhat vain-glorious terms on the part of an untried novice, they no doubt remained for contemporary audiences on the right side of the dividing-line separating stirring heroics from empty bombast.

By the sort of contrast in tone that constitutes one of the distinctive features of the tragicomedy of this period, the brisk exchanges leading to the duel are followed in scene iii by a conversation in elegiac mood. This, and the two following scenes, take place in the Infante's apartment, where Chimène has come to seek consolation. The Infante uses the conventional imagery of calm after a storm (445-46) to reassure Chimène; but her image is taken up and replaced with that of a storm resulting in shipwreck (449-51). Chimène shows herself to be much more alive to the issues involved in a quarrel between two men who are both inspired, as she knows her father and her lover to be, by the *pundonor;* line 483 echoes Rodrigue's own self-assertion in 409-10, and in lines 487-92 she reformulates as her own dilemma the moral conflict expressed by Rodrigue in the closing stanzas of I, vi: if her lover were to listen to her, and not defend his family honour, would he be worthy of her love? The Infante's practical suggestion (495-96) comes too late to be implemented: Chimène leaves full of foreboding at the news of the imminent duel, and the Infante, left with her *confidente* in scene v, gives way to a sustained flight of fancy (529-46) dictated by her wishful thinking. By now, however, we can surely recognise that the threat to the happiness of Rodrigue

and Chimène is not going to come from this source: the
Infante's role is marginal to the action, and she serves
principally to diversify the treatment of the theme of honour
and duty.

The central focus of our interest has now been clearly
defined – and formulated with almost mathematical precision
by both Rodrigue and Chimène. It is not a question of a
simple choice between love and honour (at any rate for the
young lovers themselves: as has already been seen in the case
of both fathers, the older generation is able to adopt the
simpler view). Rather, the concept of personal and family
honour is a necessary basis for love, at the same time as it
threatens that love's fulfilment.

With scene vi the location changes for the first time to the
central compartment upstage; and the King and his courtiers,
moving downstage, establish what follows as an indoor scene
at Court. The royal authority has been flouted, both in the
insult to Don Diègue and in the rejection of Don Arias's
counsel of moderation. The young Don Sanche takes up the
defence of Le Comte, interpreting his insubordination as the
result of a 'premier mouvement', or impulsive reaction; and
claims that it should be seen as the reverse of the coin to the
character's courage and *générosité*:

> Il trouve en son devoir un peu trop de rigueur,
> Et vous obéirait, s'il avait moins de cœur. (587-88)

The casuistry is apparent in the paradox; but at the same
time, in the proposition that the Comte should be allowed to
defend his individualistic defiance of legitimate authority in a
duel, we can recognise the anarchic threat posed by feudal
power to the concept of a firm centralised monarchy, and to
the new political morality which is expressed in line 602:

> Le Comte à m'obéir ne peut perdre sa gloire.

The change of subject at line 607, and the discussion of the
measures to be taken to counter the threatened attack by the
Moors, are obviously justified by the need to prepare, how-

ever perfunctorily, the events that will take place offstage between Acts III and IV. But Don Alonse returns almost immediately to announce the Count's death. At this point the exposition, and the preparation, are over: the principal action of the play, which consists of Chimène's attempt to bring Rodrigue to justice for killing her father, can now begin. We may note that first, before Chimène and Don Diègue are able to put their respective cases, the King takes the opportunity to express his own view of the affair:

> Ce que le Comte a fait semble avoir mérité
> Ce juste châtiment de sa témérité. (639-40)

Before the debate begins, then, we are given the chance to hear the objective opinion of judicial authority: *prima facie,* the Count was the guilty party, and his death was deserved.

The debate itself is launched in a vigorous scene, which begins with eight lines resembling stichomythia in their effect: an example of 'la stichomythie à forme souple', to use Jacques Scherer's term (*39,* p. 305). The two parties are competing for the King's ear, and it is only when he imposes order on this spontaneous outburst that the scene settles down to a more formal dialectical exchange. Chimène's contribution is impassioned, and she uses to good advantage both affective imagery (659-60) and rhetorical devices such as synecdoche (661ff.) and anaphora: again, we note the powerful rhetorical effect of a couplet like lines 661-62 with its high degree of identity both of sound and of sense between the two lines:

> *Ce sang qui tant de fois garantit vos murailles,*
> *Ce sang qui tant de fois vous gagna des batailles...*

The striking image of 663-64 ('Ce sang qui... fume encor de courroux / De se voir répandu pour d'autres que pour vous') is typical of the baroque sensibility of Corneille's day. Voltaire, in his *Commentaires,* was to protest that 'ces figures outrées et puériles... affaiblissent le pathétique de ce discours'; but today's readers and spectators, free from Voltaire's neoclassical prejudices, are at least able to judge such poetic figures on their own merits.

Chimène's speech is characterised by very subjective special pleading, as she tries to bring the 'raison d'état' to bear on the morality of what is really a private quarrel between two families (whereas the King's reply (671-72) implicitly emphasises the essentially domestic character of Chimène's situation). Her second speech starts with a sustained affective image ('Son sang... écrivait mon devoir... sa valeur... Me parlait par sa plaie... Par cette triste bouche...'), and shows a complete disregard for objective fact. It is disingenuous for her to claim that she is seeking vengeance 'Plus pour votre intérêt que pour mon allégeance'; and the terms 'témérité', 'jeune audacieux', betray a similarly subjective distortion. Indeed, the more one probes the logic of her plea, the more paradoxical does it appear that she should claim that

> Un si vaillant guerrier qu'on vient de vous ravir
> Eteint, s'il n'est vengé, l'ardeur de vous servir

when the Count's demeanour, as we have seen it during the play, was one verging on insubordination and rebellion. In the final lines of her speech (693-96), Chimène rises to a rhetorical climax which further underlines the emotional casuistry on which her side of the debate relies.

Don Diègue's reply is measured, sententious and dignified. He begins with what, for all their exclamatory form, are really two maxims (697-700); and the first eight lines of his speech contain a series of 'thematic' rhymes which, particularly since the second element in each case is almost predictable, provide a strong rhythmic articulation for his argument (*envie* - *vie*; *généreux* - *malheureux*; *gloire* - *victoire*; *vécu* - *vaincu*). The rhetorical devices are used here more discreetly, and to the end of intellectual, rather than emotive, persuasion; for instance, the repetition in the following couplet:

> *Ce que n'a pu jamais* combat, siège, embuscade,
> *Ce que n'a pu jamais* Aragon ni Grenade

may be contrasted with that of lines 661-62, analysed above, where the word *sang* possesses such a strong affective association; while the images (711, 712, 713, 721, etc.) for the most part belong to a conventional stock of near-clichés, much less expressive than the baroque extravagance of Chimène's opening lines (659-66). Add to this such rhetorical patterns as the ternary repetition 'digne de moi, / Digne de son pays et digne de son Roi' (715-16) and the fourfold 'Il m'a prêté sa main, il a tué le Comte, / Il m'a rendu l'honneur, il a lavé ma honte' (717-18) – where the vigour of the active verbs is attenuated by the terms *honneur* and *honte,* representative of the greater abstraction of the whole speech – and it can be seen how effective a response this controlled rejoinder makes to Chimène's passionate tirade. However, the King adjourns the debate at this point for further deliberation, and brings to a close a scene whose high seriousness anticipates the tone of Corneille's characteristic tragic style.

Act III

In Act III Rodrigue, whom we see for the first time since the death of the Comte, reacts to his unhappy situation in elegiac mood. His submissive attitude, as shown to Elvire in scene i and later to Chimène herself, and the death-wish to which he gives repeated expression (752-56, 764, and throughout the scene with Chimène) are essential 'pre-romantic' features of the role – even if the passive ill-fated lover is soon to be replaced by the more dynamic chivalric hero. For the moment, however, Rodrigue can find nothing to live for, and his purpose in visiting Chimène's house is to lay down his life at her command; though the suggestion in line 756 that the fatal 'coup' might be delivered by Chimène herself is surely a figure of speech. The speech to which this line forms the climax, with its tight construction depending on repetition (753, 754) and antithesis (752, 756), mirrors the intensity of the character's predicament; though the play on *morts / mourir* in lines 763-64 (not present in the original version of the text) is more of a superficial poetic conceit.

The other feature of the scene worthy of note is the fact that
Elvire uses *tutoiement* towards Rodrigue: an indication, perhaps, of her status as elderly family servant ('gouvernante')
enjoying certain privileges. As Chimène herself is seen arriv-
ing, Rodrigue goes into a convenient hiding-place (behind a
pillar, or a curtain? It should not be forgotten that the scene,
though conventionally supposed to take place indoors, in fact
occupied in 1637 the same stage-space as the street-scenes).
Don Sanche, who has accompanied Chimène home, fills the
role, already adumbrated in his brief intervention in II, vi, of
supporter of Don Gomès and suitor to his daughter, ready to
act as her champion; though the fact that his attentions are
unwelcome to Chimène is shown plainly enough at the
beginning of scene iii.

The tone of this scene is elegiac to begin with. Alone with
her *confidente*, Chimène can reveal what she had to hide
from the King and his courtiers: that she has been placed in a
situation that obliges her to mourn the loss of her lover as
well as that of her father. Simple in its expression, her grief is
emphasised by the affective position of the adjective (*mes
vives douleurs, mes tristes soupirs*); the discreet zeugma of
't'ouvrir mon âme et tous mes déplaisirs'; the rhetorical
repetition of 'Pleurez, pleurez... et fondez-vous...'; and the
marvellously evocative image of the following line (800) which,
with its bold metonymy, is surely one of the most memorable lines of the whole play. She will not repine in fruitless
grief, however; and the remainder of the scene gives expression to the dilemma, formulated as a counterpart to that of
Rodrigue in Act I, by which she now appeals to the audience's emotional sympathy. Chimène's speech beginning at line
810 is in its way the equivalent of Rodrigue's *stances*. There
are similar antitheses: *passion - ressentiment*; *ennemi -
amant*; *Rodrigue - mon père*, followed by the highly condensed oppositions of lines 815-16, the looser antitheses again
of *colère - flamme, cœur - âme, amour - devoir*, and the
rhetorical climax which epitomises her predicament in the
simple statement 'Rodrigue m'est bien cher... mais... mon
père est mort'. Rhyme, rhythm, balance and antithesis all work
together to produce a most effective expression of the hero-

ine's dilemma. The dilemma continues to be formulated in the 'thematic' rhymes *charmes - larmes* (833-34), *amour suborneur - honneur* (835-36) and *amoureux - généreux* (843-44); and her double appeal to her 'gloire' (842, 847) having established that she is motivated by the same demanding ethic as Rodrigue, Chimène too expresses a similar death-wish in the elegiac last line of the scene: 'le poursuivre, le perdre, et mourir après lui': a line which, although not technically a ternary alexandrine (since it possesses a clear median caesura), uses the threefold repetition of the infinitives to give affective emphasis to the character's despair in a manner not unlike that of the 'Romantic' or ternary line.

Act III scene iv is not only the central scene according to the structure of the play: it brings the lovers together for the first time, and forcefully juxtaposes the twin dilemmas of hero and heroine, thus providing an emotional high point in the plot. It also constitutes a thematic turning-point, for Rodrigue's dilemma is in the past now, his decision has been taken; the emphasis is henceforth on Chimène's situation, and any decisions rest with her. For the remainder of the play, therefore, it is she who will be the focus of our psychological interest and our sentimental sympathy. The scene insists unremittingly on the irreconcilable claims of love and honour, now shown to be working as powerfully on Chimène as they did on Rodrigue in Act I. However, it is seldom a question in Corneille's theatre of an opposition between 'masculine' honour and 'feminine' love: for Chimène as for Rodrigue, there is no doubt which is the superior claim, and Chimène too subscribes to the view that to be worthy of one's lover one must preserve the integrity of one's own honour. On the other hand, the proprieties placed more constraints on the behaviour of a young woman than on that of her lover; and it is by no means impossible for the reader or spectator of today to understand the criticism that the scene aroused on the score of the *bienséances*. For if III, iv was a major reason for the success of *Le Cid* (Act III, writes Scudéry maliciously, 'qui a fait battre des mains à tant de monde; crier miracle, à tous ceux qui ne savent pas discerner le bon or d'avec l'alchimie; et qui seul a fait la fausse réputation du *Cid'*, *8*, p. 89), it was also the occasion for serious criticism on moral grounds, not all of which can be put down to *mauvaise foi* on the part of jealous rivals of the playwright's. The fact that Chimène receives Rodrigue privately at this juncture, and the lengths to which she goes to excuse his killing of her father, called for this comment from Chapelain: 'C'est trop clairement trahir ses obligations naturelles en faveur de sa passion; c'est trop ouvertement chercher une couverture à ses désirs, et c'est faire bien moins le personnage de fille que d'amante... Que s'il eût pu être permis au poète de faire que l'un de ces deux amants préférât son amour à son devoir, on peut dire qu'il eût été plus excusable d'attribuer cette faute à Rodrigue qu'à Chimène. Rodrigue était un homme...' (*8*, pp. 373-74). Convention dictated that an unmarried girl should be reticent in the expression of her feelings towards the man she loved even at the best of times; a heroine who openly confessed her love for the man who had just killed her father was obviously making herself very vulnerable to criticism.

The provocative character of such a confrontation between the two lovers is accentuated (or at any rate, seems to a modern reader to be accentuated) by the baroque flavour of the scene. Not only is Rodrigue carrying the sword with which he has killed the Comte, but this sword, and the blood with which it is stained, are the subject of some striking word-play at the beginning of his encounter with Chimène. For the first twenty lines, which precede the more formal dialectical exchanges of lines 869 onwards, there is a remarkable concentration of imagery representing the notions of death, blood and the sword: not at all extravagant, it is true, by comparison with some of the examples of vintage baroque writing cited on pp. 14-15, but nevertheless sufficiently colourful in places to offend against the growing demand for reason and *bienséance*. Corneille was himself to comment on this feature of the scene in his *Examen* of 1660, admitting that it contained 'pensées... quelquefois trop spirituelles pour partir de personnes fort affligées', but offering the excuse that 'ces beautés étaient de mise en ce temps-là et ne le seraient plus

en celui-ci'.[17] At line 869, Rodrigue sheathes the offending
sword ('Je fais ce que tu veux'), and embarks on his moral
justification. First of all, in a six-line section whose clearly
articulated divisions follow the successive steps of the action – offence, quarrel, duel, vengeance – up to the present;
and then in a more static parenthesis, as it were (879-92),
which goes over the same ground – love versus honour, followed by the realisation that this was a false antithesis, and
that love depended on honour – as the *stances* of I, vi had
done. The third, and final, section of the speech (893ff.)
repeats insistently that Rodrigue feels no repentance for his
deed: he has done what his honour dictated, and now Chimène must take her vengeance, as her honour requires. The
latter's reply disputes neither his premise nor his conclusion.
She accepts the imperatives of *honneur* and *devoir,* for herself
as well as for Rodrigue (909, 911), and in a forceful quatrain,
in which the chiasmus of lines 914 and 916 is particularly
striking, sets the goal of her *gloire* on the same high level as
her lover's. In a series of paradoxes and antithetical proposi-
tions, lightened only by the wistful thoughts of what might
have been 'Si quelque autre malheur m'avait ravi mon père...'
(917-22), she reaffirms her resolve. Lines 927-28 take up the
terms in which Rodrigue had refused to repent of his action
(871-72), and her speech closes with the sublime paradox of
lines 931-32:

> Tu t'es, en m'offensant, montré digne de moi;
> Je me dois, par ta mort, montrer digne de toi.

Rodrigue's persistence, exhorting Chimène not to wait for
the slower processes of justice, but to avenge her father then
and there (937-39, 947-50, 959-62, 967-68) is presumably
what Nadal has in mind in his comment on the 'blackmail-
ing' of Chimène by her lover (*32,* p. 170). Rodrigue's own
sword is now sheathed, and his language no longer contains

---

[17] On the other hand, the text of this scene is changed hardly at all from
the 1637 version to later editions.

the vivid imagery of the beginning of the scene; but there is
something characteristically baroque in this repeated appeal
by a lover for death at his mistress's hands, whether one takes
it literally or as a means of forcing her to confess her inability
to act out the logic of her position. Such is certainly the effect
of this series of exchanges; and far from provoking Chimène
to resentment and retaliation, Rodrigue's insistence produces
the clearest statement of her continuing love for him. She has
previously spoken in more guarded terms of 'une main si
chère' (922) and of her 'affection' (927): now she not only
admits she is powerless to hate her father's killer (963), but
throwing away all maidenly reserve, she proclaims that her
gloire demands that it be known 'que je t'adore et que je te
poursuis' (972). And in lines 982-84 she makes a lucid
admission that goes a long way towards accepting – indeed,
welcoming – the eventual need for surrender: 'Je ferai mon
possible... Mais... Mon unique souhait est de ne rien pouvoir'.

The last twenty lines of the scene are a marvellously
lyrical expression of a shared love, paradoxically able to
express itself freely only now that it is under such a terrible
threat. The exclamatory exaltation of lines 985, 987, 991; the
conventional – but no less effective – image of hope ship-
wrecked within sight of the harbour (989-90); the simple but
evocative parallel expressions of a romantic death-wish
(993-94, 995-96) are rounded off by the intimate, homely
touch of Chimène's 'garde bien qu'on te voie', and by the
sublimely elegiac note of the couplet with which the scene
closes when the heroine is left alone with her *confidente.*
Here, the effect depends partly on the thematic rhyme *soupi-
rer - pleurer,* and partly on the structure of the final line,
where the hendiadys, 'le silence et la nuit' (so much more
striking than the normal 'le silence de la nuit', 'la nuit
silencieuse') cuts across the caesura to produce an effect not
unlike that of the Romantic ternary alexandrine.

As Nadal writes, a meeting between the lovers so soon
after the fatal duel, as well as offending against contemporary
notions of *bienséance,* was contrary to all common sense; but
'Corneille se sentait pressé par une nécessité plus impérieuse

que les règles, par une vérité plus vraie que la vie même' (*32*, p. 168). Few students of the play will be inclined to disagree with this: there can surely be no doubt as to the *aesthetic* justification of such a meeting, and Act III scene iv is a tribute to the independence of judgement which enabled the dramatist to emancipate himself from the rationalistic pedantry of some of his contemporaries.

After the brief linking scene v, we come to the first encounter between father and son since the family honour has been avenged. Scene vi is dramatically interesting, first and foremost, because of the conflict of ideas between the two characters: on the one hand, an exclusive ideological commitment to the notion of family honour and pride, to which all more humane feelings are ruthlessly subordinated, on the other a reluctant acknowledgement of these imperatives, indissolubly bound up with the recognition of their cost on an ordinary human level. [18] In terms of dramatic style, the contrast is striking between Don Diègue's emotional fervour, symbolised in his invitation to his son to kiss the cheek whose shame Rodrigue's courage has now purged, and the latter's reply which not only fails to match his father's exalted eloquence, but explicitly criticises (1051-52) the limited ethic of the *pundonor*. Don Diègue encourages his son in the name of *gloire* (1054) and *magnanimité* (1057) to rise above ('porte plus haut', 1053) his personal preoccupations; but the two characters remain on quite different wavelengths, as it were. Although the ideological abstractions expressed by the father in the *sentences* of lines 1058-59 are countered in similar vein by the son in his generalised proposition of lines 1063-64, Rodrigue is not really motivated by such general considerations, as is shown by the predominance of the first-person pronoun and possessive adjective in the rest of his reply which frames this maxim (1061-62, 1065-70). His

[18] Although this conflict appears to be based in *Le Cid* on a difference of generation – the two fathers contrasted with a son and daughter – Corneille's next play, *Horace,* features a very similar opposition between two young men; while Horace shares his father's single-minded ideological commitment, Curiace obeys his patriotic duty reluctantly, alive to its cost in human terms.

mood is elegiac, and the speech finishes with a repetition of
the death-wish he had already expressed in the scene with
Chimène, poetically heightened by a *reprise* of the rhyme
Chimène - peine from the *stances* of Act I, coupled with the
striking oxymoron of 'ma plus douce peine'.

'Le trépas que je cherche' allows Don Diègue a natural
change of subject. The imminent arrival of the Moors, and
Rodrigue's night battle with the enemy, have often been
criticised both on the grounds that the packed timetable of
events strains credulity, and as producing a new and unforeseen development in the plot. As Corneille himself admits in
his *Examen,* the fact that the Moors 'se présentent d'eux-
mêmes, sans être appelés dans la pièce, directement ni indi-
rectement, par aucun acteur du premier acte' is a structural
blemish; and I think that this must be the case even for
twentieth-century spectators with a more flexible approach to
such matters. The mention of the Moors in II, vi (607ff.) does
not go very far towards preparing us for their arrival, and
what we have here is a new 'péril' for the hero which does not
arise as a consequence of the first. Corneille was later to
criticise the structure of *Horace* because the hero of that play
was subjected to two distinct 'périls'; but *Le Cid* is an even
more notable case of this, for as the playwright himself writes:
'Les Maures viennent dans *Le Cid* après la mort du Comte, et
non pas à cause de la mort du Comte' (*Discours des trois
unités*), and this feature of the play thus offends against the
Aristotelian precept that 'tout ce qui se passe dans la tragédie
doit arriver nécessairement ou vraisemblablement de ce qui
l'a précédé'.

ACT IV

The last two scenes of Act III have taken us out of doors,
after the supposed indoor location of the first part of this act,
to which we now return at the beginning of Act IV. Here, two
consecutive scenes in Chimène's apartment focus on the
heroine's predicament. Her spontaneous delight at the news
of Rodrigue's achievements makes her admiration clear

(1110, 1113, 1117); but as soon as her concern for his safety has been satisfied (1123-24), she at once reaffirms her deter- mination not to give way to affective impulse. The speech beginning at line 1125 is an excellent example of what Scherer (quoting Corneille himself) means by passages 'à grande pompe' (*39,* pp. 297-98). The noble purpose is expres- sed by a striking series of thematic rhymes: *colère - père; malheur - valeur; magnanime - crime; ressentiments - orne- ments; victoire - gloire; pouvoir - devoir;* and the speech is punctuated by the strong antitheses '(reprenez vos esprits) // Reprenons... ma colère'; 'S'il a vaincu deux rois, // il a tué mon père'; 'Contre ma passion // soutenez bien ma gloire' – the last of these lines being the climax of a rhetorical 'quatrain' in which (as later Cornelian characters will do at moments of emotional crisis)[19] Chimène apostrophises the tangible symbols of her grief.

On the Infante's entry, this rhetorical exaltation gives way to a realistic appreciation of Rodrigue's services to the state, and of Chimène's own exclusion from the general rejoicing, by turns ironic (1145-47, 1154-56) and wistful (1164), before concluding with another of the play's most memorable poetic images in this climax to a powerfully elegiac quatrain:

> J'irai sous mes cyprès accabler ses lauriers.

The role of the Infante in scene ii is almost entirely reduced to that of *confidente* to Chimène. Not quite, though, for in her pleas 'Ote-lui ton amour, mais laisse-nous sa vie' (1190) and 'c'est assez que d'éteindre ta flamme' (1201) there must be seen to be an element of self-interest and wishful thinking on the Princess's part. However, the scene closes with Chi- mène's firm rejection of this alternative.

For scene iii we return to the King's council-chamber. It is a scene which contains an outstanding *tour de force* in the narrative of the battle against the Moors which, though it may perhaps be less to the taste of modern spectators or

---

[19] For instance Cornélie's opening speech in V, i of *Pompée.*

readers, must have been one of the principal attractions of the play for its first audiences. Its 82 lines make Rodrigue's *récit* shorter than many other narratives of off-stage action in the seventeenth-century theatre (Théramène's account of Hippolyte's death in *Phèdre* runs to 90 lines, and *récits* in Corneille's own *Cinna* and *Pompée* both exceed the 100-line mark). What does distinguish this scene in *Le Cid,* however, is that the narrative is delivered by the principal participant in the event and not, as is usually the case, by a spectator in the form of a secondary character or *confident.* Indeed, it constitutes one of the major technical challenges to the actor playing Rodrigue, revealing as it does, shrewdly observes Maurice Descotes, 'la nécessité d'un comédien de souffle et non de composition, car la narration du combat n'apporte aucun élément nouveau à la construction psychologique du héros'. It is the 'beauté d'ensemble' of the speech that counts, says Descotes, not its 'beautés de détail'; and the actor must be 'lui-même emporté par le rythme du récit' if he is to carry the audience with him (*21,* p. 65).

The King's opening salutation establishes an elevated tone with such stylistic features as the reiterated latinisms of construction in lines 1215-17 and, as regards subject-matter, the reported homage of the captive Moors to their young conqueror, who is now to be known as 'Le Cid': a 'beau titre d'honneur' that we perhaps take somewhat for granted, though its significance of course derives from these lines. Rodrigue's own preamble is devoted to excusing himself for his audacity in assuming command of the King's troops, while Fernand's reply closely prefigures the argument of the final scene: Chimène's judicial pursuit of her lover has even less chance of succeeding now he has become the principal defender of the state.

Even if it is, as Descotes suggests, the rhythm and impetus of the *récit* that matter most, the speech is by no means uniform in tone; and alongside the more properly epic, or narrative, qualities that characterise the vigorous account of the battle itself – prominence of the active verb, frequency of a paratactic succession of main clauses, anaphora, and the use of a strong caesura for reinforcement or balance – there also stand out contrasting features such as the striking evocation of the stillness of the night and the silent arrival of the enemy, in which oxymoron, metonymy and zeugma combine to produce a masterpiece of lyrical expression:

> Cette obscure clarté qui tombe des étoiles
> Enfin avec le flux nous fait voir trente voiles;
> L'onde s'enfle dessous, et d'un commun effort
> Les Mores et la mer montent jusques au port.

Overall, however, the pace of the passage is swift and dynamic, reflecting Rodrigue's martial mood; and memorable lines such as 'Le flux les apporta, le reflux les remporte' or 'Et le combat cessa faute de combattants' successfully convey the buoyant self-confidence of the young hero celebrating his triumph with a virtuoso recital of the event.

By another of the contrasts of tone which characterise the style of baroque drama (and establish one of its closest links with our own Elizabethan and Jacobean theatre), the next sequence (comprising scene iv and the beginning of scene v) descends to the level of comedy, as the King tricks Chimène – the device is borrowed from Guillén de Castro – into betraying her feelings. But while Don Diègue is prepared to play the same game, Chimène indignantly rejects such behaviour; and her speech beginning at line 1355 at once raises the tone by the vehemence of her rhetoric. This is the public face of Chimène: we have seen her private feelings in the love-duet of lines 963-97, but in the presence of King and Court she maintains an unyielding demand for vengeance. It is a well-structured speech, and its logical articulation is supported by such emphatic features as the thrice-repeated 'non pas...' of lines 1362-64, the *sentence* of lines 1367-68 (which will recur almost unchanged in *Horace*), and strong thematic rhymes (*crime - victime*; *guerriers - lauriers*). The King's replies show his weakness and lack of authority: he tries to avoid recourse to judicial combat, of which he says he has always disapproved (1451-52), but his 'J'en dispense Rodrigue' (1411) is no more than the arbitrary application of 'la raison d'état'; and when this is pointed out by Don Diègue

(1415ff.), he weakly changes his mind.[20] Again, at the end of the scene, he is equally ready to modify his proposal that the duel should take place 'à demain' with the feeble 'Du moins une heure ou deux je veux qu'il se délasse'. This little exchange, with its obtrusive reminder of unity of time, is surely unnecessary; while Don Diègue's 'Rodrigue a pris haleine en vous la racontant' is frankly comic. The picture of hesitant and uncertain kingship is derived from Corneille's source in Castro's play; but in the heroic idiom of *Le Cid* the presence of Don Fernand (and even that of Don Diègue) all too often indicates a descent to the more familiar manner of comedy.

Act V

Act V begins with a scene in Chimène's house, which again shows us the private face of the heroine. It is very much a *reprise* of III, v, with the same concern for her reputation on the part of Chimène (1465-66), followed by a renewed expression of a death-wish by the lover who has offended his mistress and has nothing left to live for. The strength of this scene lies in its insistent concentration on a few simple themes. For the most part it maintains the same tone of elegiac lament as its predecessor, with both lovers making the most of the dialectical interplay between the ideas of love and honour, life and death. Chimène's challenge of lines 1521-22:

> Va, sans vouloir mourir, laisse-moi te poursuivre,
> Et défends ton honneur, si tu ne veux plus vivre

prompts Rodrigue's sublime response – sublime, that is, as an expression of the heroic ethos to which Corneille expects his spectators to subscribe:

> Pour venger son honneur il perdit son amour,
> Pour venger sa maîtresse il a quitté le jour,

[20] On the theme of 'raison d'état' in Corneille's early plays, see *25*.

> Préférant, quelque espoir qu'eût son âme asservie,
> Son honneur à Chimène, et Chimène à sa vie. (1539-42)

However, unlike their earlier encounter, this meeting ends on a note of positive resolution. Since it seems that only a completely unequivocal encouragement will persuade Rodrigue not to sacrifice his life, Chimène is forced to make a complete abdication of her public stance as her father's implacable avenger:

> ... va, songe à ta défense,
> Pour forcer mon devoir, pour m'imposer silence;
> Et si tu sens pour moi ton cœur encor épris,
> Sors vainqueur d'un combat dont Chimène est le prix.

Rodrigue's exultant soliloquy, with which this scene ends, might, if one were to take it out of context, appear to be yet another example of bombastic extravagance. But even the hyperbole of lines 1561-62, with their echo of Matamore:

> ... faites-vous une armée,
> Pour combattre une main de la sorte animée

is completely justified by the psychological context. The triumphant outburst does not signify arrogance, but buoyant resolve fortified by a reciprocated love: these heroic lines form a fitting climax to the lovers' meeting, and a prelude to the final sequence of scenes. [21]

However, before the final scenes which focus on the solution to Chimène's dilemma, we have two scenes which have been much criticised as contributing nothing to the action, and diluting the final build-up of suspense. Scenes ii and iii return us to the Infante's apartments, and invite us to interest ourselves once more in this minor character, whose concerns are now more marginal than ever to the major

---

[21] A remark in Voltaire's commentary on this scene indicates that by his day the practice had grown up of omitting these lines in performance (*10*, Vol. II, p. 79).

dramatic and emotional focus of the play. Voltaire wondered at this point how Corneille could bear to bring back 'notre pitoyable Infante'; and the principal justification of these scenes seems to be a dramaturgical one: the desire to fill the interval necessary for the fighting of the duel, and so avoid producing a temporal hiatus within an act. The content of the two scenes contributes little of either psychological or dramatic importance to the play: the static *stances,* which examine the Princess's dilemma in an indecisive and inconclusive manner, are followed by a scene with her *confidente* in which she appears to contradict herself quite arbitrarily. For having concluded the soliloquy by recognising that the real obstacle to her happiness is not her royal birth, which prevents her marriage to a mere 'gentilhomme', but the fact that Rodrigue and Chimène still love each other, she now proposes to override this ('en rompre l'effet') by resorting to a jealous lover's 'inventions' (1608) and 'artifices' (1610) – only to revert a few lines later to the affirmation of her magnanimity: 'Je ne veux point reprendre un bien que j'ai donné' (1640). In any case, the truth of the matter surely is that magnanimous renunciation and threatened rivalry are equally irrelevant, and these two scenes must be counted as weak in both invention and expression.

With scene iv we return to Chimène's house. Although this scene too helps to fill the time-interval, Chimène's emotional state is of much greater interest to us, and her hesitations over the outcome of the duel are in any case much more plausibly motivated. Caught here for the last time in private self-interrogation (effectively helped along by Elvire's prompting), her only wish is to reconcile two equally deeply-felt emotions. Whoever triumphs in the duel, the consequences will be unbearable; and the reader or spectator ought to be persuaded by now that this is not merely a question of 'love' versus 'duty'. What is involved is the conflict between two instinctive feelings:

> De tous les deux côtés on me donne un mari
> Encor tout teint du sang que j'ai le plus chéri (1659-60)

– and her only futile hope, as is shown by her despairing prayer, is that such an outcome might be avoided by deferring the resolution of the conflict:

> ... Toi, puissant moteur du destin qui m'outrage,
> Termine ce combat sans aucun avantage,
> Sans faire aucun des deux ni vaincu ni vainqueur. (1665-67)

In short, Act V scene iv provides a further demonstration that the effect of the emotional crisis, while it has strengthened Rodrigue's resolve and justified his decisions, has been to underline the vulnerability of Chimène's position and to point the contrast between her public confidence and her private state of doubt and indecision. However, Elvire's robust common sense does finally have the effect of forcing her mistress to acknowledge (1700-03) that if she is obliged to choose, the prospect of marriage to Don Sanche is more thoroughly repugnant to her; and it is upon this skilfully managed climax to the scene that Sanche himself arrives, bearing his sword.

Scene v is another that has attracted criticism, from the time of the 'Querelle du Cid' onwards. The misunderstanding which leads Chimène to reveal her love publicly in the following scene is too much like a comic device; it comes too near to repeating the pattern of IV, iv - v, where the King had set up his deliberate deception of her; and it lasts too long, since Chimène interrupts Don Sanche no fewer than three times, preventing him from putting the record straight. In its 1637 version, the scene was nearly twice as long: Corneille evidently made some effort to reduce the effect of a too long drawn out *quiproquo*, though in doing so he chose to cut out the most interesting contribution of the scene in its original form from a psychological point of view: two passages in which Chimène contemplates suicide as the only means of avoiding marriage to Don Sanche.

The location of scenes vi and vii has long been a subject of critical dispute. Put briefly, the problem is this: does Chimène proceed to the Court between scenes v and vi, or does the King visit her at home? I will return to the question in a later chapter: let me say briefly at this point that the only satisfactory interpretation of the sequence of events in the 1637 version of the text, in my view, is that scene vi is intended to carry straight on from scene v without a break, and therefore must likewise take place in Chimène's house, where Fernand and the Court come to visit her. I see no reason to adopt a different interpretation when we come to the 1660 text, where a break between scenes v and vi would be equally difficult to justify. It must be admitted, however, that this view is not shared by a number of modern editors and commentators. The Bordas edition, for instance, distinguishes between scenes iv and v ('chez Chimène') and scenes vi and vii ('chez le Roi'); while Nurse follows Scherer in assuming that there is a change of location between scenes v and vi of the 1660 version, even if that had not been the case in 1637 (*3*, p. 27; *2*, p. 31). However, the only argument in favour of a change of location seems to be based on the view that it would not be consistent with protocol for a monarch to visit a subject's house. In the absence of any conclusive indication in the text itself, dramatic logic appears to point in the other direction; and in the case of the original *mise en scène* this is supported by external evidence, since Scudéry, commenting on the beginning of scene vi, writes: 'Comme ils en sont là, le Roi et toute la Cour arrive' (*8*, p. 95).

Once Chimène's misinterpretation of Don Sanche's message has been cleared up, her defences are largely broken down. There can be no going back after the public revelation of 'Ce que tous mes efforts ne vous ont pu celer' (1724); and significantly she remains silent while others speak; the King, in a firm, fatherly tone, preparing the way for his final proposal at the denouement. 'Ta gloire est dégagée, et ton devoir est quitte' (1766): this is no doubt the official view of what Chimène owed to family honour, and as Don Fernand suggests, 'mettre tant de fois ton Rodrigue en danger' (1768) is an entirely adequate response to the challenge that she has had to face, in the eyes of the public. But as Corneille's later plays were so abundantly to demonstrate, *la gloire* has a private as well as a public aspect: reputation in the world's eyes is not everything, and what one owes to oneself is even more

important. Thus, while the King's verdict will satisfy every-
one else, Chimène herself cannot be satisfied with outward
appearances and observances. It is this debate between the
public and the private faces of the heroine's *gloire* that will
give the final scene its full import, and help to solve the
riddle of the meaning of the denouement. With the entrance
of Rodrigue at line 1773 everything is prepared for the
emotional and ideological climax of the play.

The Infante's arrival with Rodrigue at the beginning of
scene vii shows Corneille concerned to leave no loose ends.
This character has long since ceased to pose a threat to the
lovers' happiness, but lines 1773-74 mark the definitive
abandonment of the rival claim to Rodrigue. He, however,
has no more time for her irrelevant generosity than have we,
and he launches at once into a direct appeal to Chimène
which combines heroic *élan* with emotional exaltation. Re-
fusing the advantage of the King's authority and of his own
prowess at arms, he offers to undergo whatever further tests
she may impose; his speech contains echoes of the mediaeval
trial by combat, and the deference to his mistress's will
typical of the courtly tradition, together with pre-echoes of
the confident self-affirmation that will be characteristic of so
many Cornelian *généreux*. Once again, as with lines 1561-62,
this is not vainglorious boasting, and the hyperbole of 1783-86
is perfectly acceptable in the mouth of a young warrior who
has just earned the title of 'Cid'. The plea that follows: in
effect, that Chimène should show herself his equal by executing
her own vengeance, is not unlike the emotional blackmail we
encounter in some of Corneille's later plays: there is no
chance now (indeed, there never has been) of Chimène taking
vengeance into her own hands, but the heroic ultimatum (she
alone can 'vaincre un invincible', 1793) is the necessary
introduction to the splendid pathetic climax of 'S'il ne
m'avait aimée, il ne serait pas mort'.

Chimène's speech at line 1801 contains the most important textual changes of the whole play; and it is here above all
that, if we are to succeed in understanding the reception of *Le
Cid* by its first audiences, priority must be given to the text of
1637.

Her opening 'Relève-toi, Rodrigue' maintains the convention established as the norm in the previous meetings between
the two characters: III, iv which, though it was to move into
'tutoiement passionné', had nevertheless begun with the use
of the *vous* form by the lover to his mistress, who responded
with the more familiar *tu*; and V, i in which adhered completely to this courtly convention. However, after this initial
half-line, the rest of Chimène's speech is addressed to the
King; and the 1637 text establishes an emphasis which has
disappeared from that of the 1660 edition. Lines 1831-34 of
the original version (corresponding to 1805-08 of the revised
text) read as follows:

> Mais, à quoi que déjà vous m'ayez condamnée,
> Sire, quelle apparence, à ce triste hyménée,
> Qu'un même jour commence et finisse mon deuil,
> Mette en mon lit Rodrigue et mon père au cercueil?

In this version, it can at once be seen that Chimène's protest
is directed exclusively against the *immediate* conclusion of
the marriage ('un même jour ...'), an objection to which the
King's reply makes specific, and adequate, response ('Le
temps assez souvent a rendu légitime / Ce qui semblait
d'abord ne se pouvoir sans crime...'). Conceding that Chimène's objection is a reasonable one, Fernand meets it with
an equally reasonable proposal that Rodrigue should return
to claim her in marriage in a year's time, when he will have
further conquests to his name. The implications of the textual
revision at this point will be examined in a later chapter: as
regards the original text of 1637, there can surely be no room
for doubt that it implied a 'happy ending'. We are meant to
assume, with the King, that the delay of a year will satisfy
Chimène's legitimate objection to immediate marriage, and
that after this interval the hero and heroine will be united. This
is entirely in keeping with the ethos of heroic tragicomedy to
which Corneille and his 1637 audiences subscribed; and the
whole logical development of this final scene – Rodrigue's
offer to lay down his life; Chimène's refusal to accept his
offer, pleading only that the marriage be not concluded then

and there; the King's granting of a year's delay; Rodrigue's enthusiastic acceptance – leaves no ambiguity about the outcome. The morality of the heroine's agreeing to marry the man who has killed her father was to be one of the principal issues of the 'Querelle du Cid': the fact that the marriage will take place (after a year's delay) was at this stage apparently never questioned, and at a date at which much greater demands than this were constantly being made on the credulity of spectators and readers, in both the theatre and the novel of the day, any reservations about the psychological plausibility of Chimène's implied assent were hardly likely to jeopardise acceptance of the heroic exaltation with which the play concludes.

4

The 'Querelle du Cid'

T H E documents constituting the literary controversy over *Le Cid* which erupted in the immediate aftermath of the play were published by Armand Gasté in 1898 (see *8*); this volume, or its modern reprint, is readily available in libraries, and it is to this edition that reference will be made. Gasté brought together no fewer than 36 texts from a variety of hands, two of which stand out from the remainder both in terms of their substantial size and by virtue of their critical comment: the *Observations sur le Cid* by Georges de Scudéry, a rival playwright (his tragedy *La Mort de César* had been performed in 1635), and the *Sentiments de l'Académie Française sur la tragicomédie du Cid* drawn up by Jean Chapelain, one of the founding members of the Academy, and published by him on behalf of that body. For the rest, the level of critical debate is pretty low, and the content of the various contributions to the Querelle very repetitive, the controversy being fuelled on both sides by professional jealousy and personal animosity, much of it of a remarkably petty nature. Corneille must bear his share of the blame for this, for it was the boastful *Excuse à Ariste* which produced a sharp response from other poets and playwrights. This initial piece purports to be Corneille's reply to a request from a friend, père André de Saint-Denis, to send him some light verse set to music. The constraints of such artificial composition do not suit his genius, the playwright claims; he is at home only in his chosen medium of dramatic verse; and his 'Excuse' turns into a provocative piece of self-advertisement:

> Je satisfais ensemble et peuple et courtisans
> Et mes vers en tous lieux sont mes seuls partisans.

Par leur seule beauté ma plume est estimée;
Je ne dois qu'à moi seul toute ma renommée,
Et pense toutefois n'avoir point de rival
A qui je fasse tort en le traitant d'égal.   (8, p. 64)

Other poets were quick to rise to the provocation. Jean Mairet, author of the tragedy *Sophonisbe* (1634), was first in the field with *L'Auteur du vrai Cid espagnol à son traducteur français* in which, under the pseudonym Don Balthasar de la Verdad (= 'Truth'), he accuses Corneille of plagiarism, maintaining that the beauties of *Le Cid* are stolen beauties, and that the playwright will be a sorry sight (a 'Corneille déplumée') when he has been forced to shed his borrowed plumage. Corneille's answer to this was in the stylised form of a fifteen-line *rondeau*, in which Mairet's muse is despatched to the brothel:

Paris entier, ayant lu son cartel,
L'envoie au diable, et sa muse au bordel.   (p. 70)

Indicative though this sort of exchange may be of the vanity and susceptibility of the personalities involved, it hardly serves to establish the 'Querelle du Cid' as a major literary controversy; and it must be said that few of the contributions rise above this level. It is, however, worth looking in rather more detail at Scudéry's *Observations* and at the *Sentiments de l'Académie*.

The *Observations* make no secret of Scudéry's hostility towards Corneille; and this text (of forty pages in Gasté's edition) is a laboured and pedantic exercise in criticism for criticism's sake, devoted to the following proposition:

... je prétends donc prouver contre cette pièce du Cid,
    que le sujet n'en vaut rien du tout,
    qu'il choque les principales règles du poème dramatique,
    qu'il manque de jugement en sa conduite,
    qu'il a beaucoup de méchants vers,
    que presque tout ce qu'il a de beautés sont dérobées,
    et qu'ainsi l'estime qu'on en fait est injuste.   (p. 73)

The last two items in this indictment in particular show the
pedantry that is typical not merely of Scudéry's method, but of
neo-classical literary criticism generally (Voltaire's manner in
his *Commentaires sur Corneille,* for instance, is hardly more
enlightened). The text is combed for expressions that can be
denounced as departures from current French usage; poetic
licence is condemned out of hand in the name of reason
and common sense; and plagiarism is pursued with narrow-
minded zeal. Elsewhere, however, Scudéry has more to offer
the modern reader, as he focuses on the issues which give the
reception of *Le Cid* such an absorbing historical interest: that
is to say, the evolution from baroque tragicomedy, and the
aesthetic of the multiple set, to classical tragedy, the fixed
perspective set, and the unities of time and place. Some of
Scudéry's comments are a little disingenuous, for Corneille's
practice was very much that of his contemporaries in this
transitional period. Essentially, however, what he is saying
– though not explicitly in these terms – is that while Corneille
has meticulously observed the unities, the external features of
his plot with its eventful detail would have been better suited
to the episodic treatment characteristic of tragicomedy:

> Véritablement toutes ces belles actions que fit le Cid en plu-
> sieurs années sont tellement assemblées par force en cette
> pièce pour les mettre dans les vingt-quatre heures, que les per-
> sonnages y semblent des dieux de machine qui tombent du
> ciel en terre: car enfin, dans le court espace d'un jour naturel,
> on élit un gouverneur au Prince de Castille; il se fait une que-
> relle et un combat entre Don Diègue et le Comte, autre combat
> de Rodrigue et du Comte, un autre de Rodrigue contre les
> Mores; un autre contre Don Sanche; et le mariage se conclut,
> entre Rodrigue et Chimène: je vous laisse à juger, si ne voilà
> pas un jour bien employé, et si l'on n'aurait pas grand tort
> d'accuser tous ces personnages de paresse?   (pp. 77-78)

Similarly, as regards unity of place:

> Le théâtre [de cette pièce] est si mal entendu, qu'un même
> lieu, représentant l'appartement du Roi, celui de l'Infante, la

> maison de Chimène et la rue, presque sans changer de face, le
> spectateur ne sait le plus souvent où sont les acteurs. (p. 95)

At the same time, Scudéry's criticisms on the score of the
moral tone, or *bienséance,* of the play illustrate, however per-
fidious his purpose may have been, the contemporary evolution from the aesthetic requirements of pure romanesque
entertainment towards a concept of drama based on psychological coherence and moral instruction. Here, it is of course
the case of Chimène's continuing love for (and the prospect of
her marriage to) the man who has killed her father that is the
subject of the weightiest criticism:

> La vertu semble bannie de la conclusion de ce poème; il est
> une instruction au mal, un aiguillon pour nous y pousser; et
> par ces fautes remarquables et dangereuses, directement op-
> posé aux principales règles dramatiques. (p. 80)

It was with plays like this in mind, Scudéry continues, that
Plato banned imaginative writing from his ideal republic; and
it is interesting to see him opt, when faced with the choice
that was to play such an important role in neo-classical
theory, for *le vraisemblable* rather than *le vrai*:

> Ces grands maîtres anciens, qui m'ont appris ce que je montre
> ici à ceux qui l'ignorent, nous ont toujours enseigné que le
> poète et l'historien ne doivent pas suivre la même route: et
> qu'il vaut mieux que le premier traite un sujet vraisemblable,
> qui ne soit pas vrai, qu'un vrai qui ne soit pas vraisemblable...
> C'est pourquoi j'ajoute... qu'il est vrai que Chimène épousa le
> Cid, mais qu'il n'est point vraisemblable qu'une fille d'hon-
> neur épouse le meurtrier de son père. Cet événement était bon
> pour l'historien, mais il ne valait rien pour le poète. (p. 75)

This was to be Boileau's doctrine ('Le vrai peut quelquefois
n'être pas vraisemblable');[22] and it was to be central to Racine's practice. Corneille's classicism, on the other hand, re-

---

[22] *Art poétique,* III, 48.

mained heterodox in this, as in certain other respects; and throughout his career he was continually to seek the extraordinary subject with the guarantee of historical truth.[23]

Scudéry's *Observations,* then, have the merit of raising fundamental aesthetic issues, even if the focus is somewhat blurred by pedantry and personal rancour. It was Scudéry too, in further interventions in the Querelle, who urged that the controversy over *Le Cid* should be referred to the Academy's arbitration.

Richelieu's role in this referral will no doubt always be a matter for debate. A legend, whose origins go back to the middle of the seventeenth century, has it that when Corneille broke away from the 'Compagnie des cinq auteurs' and claimed independence from the Cardinal and his immediate entourage, this angered his authoritarian patron; and that Richelieu's displeasure was further increased by the success of *Le Cid,* a play that was not wholly in line with the move towards regular drama championed by the Cardinal, moreover a play with a Spanish subject (during a period of war with Spain), and one which glorified duelling (in the aftermath of Richelieu's attempts to stamp it out). The notion of a Richelieu 'jealous' of Corneille's success and determined to punish him for it, first put out by Pellisson and Tallemant in the 1650s and 1660s,[24] was quite widely accepted by the generation of Boileau and La Bruyère, and was to be further reinforced by such later comments as that by Corneille's nephew, Fontenelle, who wrote in 1729: 'Quand *Le Cid* parut, le Cardinal en fut aussi alarmé que s'il avait vu les Espagnols devant Paris'. Such a view, however, surely rests on an anachronistic picture of the 1630s. Whereas the perspective of the modern literary historian can acknowledge Richelieu and Corneille as two of the greatest figures of their age, this cannot have been the case in 1637, when a comparison on any-

---

[23] 'Je ne craindrai pas d'avancer que le sujet d'une belle tragédie doit n'être pas vraisemblable' (*Examen* to *Héraclius*).

[24] Tallemant, with typical exaggeration, writes: 'Il eut une jalousie enragée contre *Le Cid,* à cause que ses pièces des Cinq Auteurs n'avaient pas trop bien réussi' (*Historiettes,* ed. A. Adam, Paris, Gallimard, 1960, I, p. 272).

thing like an equal footing between the powerful Cardinal-Minister and one of his 'poètes à gages' would have been utterly absurd.

The facts appear in any case to support a different hypothesis; and without going so far as to suggest, with Batiffol and Lacour (see *15, 26*), that the legend of Richelieu's hostility is quite without foundation, I believe it is possible to reconcile these facts with a more plausible view of the preoccupations of a busy statesman. It seems clear that Richelieu took an interest in *Le Cid,* and that this initial interest may well have been favourable, even if it fell short of Lacour's suggestion that 'le ministre sentit si bien les beautés neuves du *Cid* qu'il en fut désormais, comme dramaturge, la proie' (*26,* p. 15). We know that, in addition to its enormous success at the Marais, the play was performed three times at Court, and twice at the Hôtel Richelieu; that the *privilège* for the publication of *Le Cid* was authorised in an exceptionally short time, and that when it appeared in March 1637 the play was dedicated to Richelieu's favourite niece, Madame de Combalet; that Corneille was given a sizeable pension on Richelieu's private list in 1637, and that letters patent granting nobility to Corneille's father and his family date from the same year; while it is also possible that Richelieu's intervention helped to expedite the poet's marriage-settlement in 1638. All of this suggests benevolence on the Cardinal's part rather than the opposite. On the other hand, he could not possibly remain completely detached from the cabals and intrigues which were already a feature of the literary scene before *Le Cid,* and which, on that play's appearance, promptly divided the world of letters into supporters and adversaries of Corneille. The latter's independence, his resignation from the Cinq Auteurs, the arrogance of the *Excuse à Ariste* all provide sufficient explanation for the concerted attacks on *Le Cid*; and since the group of writers supported by Richelieu were almost without exception hostile to Corneille – and two in particular, Boisrobert and d'Aubignac, seem to have been actively involved in stirring up the controversy – one hardly needs to look much further for the reason for the Cardinal's behaviour at the time of the Querelle.

What is certain is that Richelieu responded positively to
Scudéry's suggestion, welcoming the proposal that the new
body of literary legislators should demonstrate its capabil-
ities on an issue of immediate consequence to a wide public.
The Academicians accepted reluctantly; it was in any case
contrary to the Academy's statutes to engage in criticism of a
contemporary work against the author's wishes, but Corneille, who had little choice in the matter, consented with a
not very good grace. A number of *commissaires* were desig-
nated; but it was soon agreed that Chapelain should undertake
the task on his colleagues' behalf, and having begun the work
in June 1637, he published the *Sentiments* in December. In
the meantime, a first draft had been presented to the Academy, who approved it, and to Richelieu, who asked for
certain changes. Whereas Batiffol claims that Richelieu's
intention was to modify Chapelain's hostility towards Corneille, other scholars who have examined the evidence are
agreed that in this instance at least the legend of Richelieu's
own hostility is not without foundation, and that his intervention had the effect of hardening the critical tone of the *Sentiments* (cf. *7; 11,* vol. I, pp. 513-18). Meanwhile, before publication of the Academy's verdict, contributions to the Querelle had become steadily more scurrilous: comments were
exchanged on the birth and breeding of participants, and
certain texts even descended to threats of physical violence.
While one modern commentator may be able to conclude
that the Querelle shows Corneille's 'talent supérieur de polé-
miste' (*37,* p. 307), it also seems undeniable that he was the
aggressor at a less elevated level of personal invective. At all
events, in October 1637 the element of scandal in the controversy was so great that Richelieu moved swiftly to bring it to
an end, making his wishes known through Boisrobert as
intermediary both to Corneille and to Mairet, his principal
adversary.

The *Sentiments de l'Académie,* though not inspired by the
same animosity against the author of *Le Cid* as the *Observations,* nevertheless embody, at least in their published form, a
different form of hostility to the play itself, less personal but
equally uncompromising. Indeed, it is a characteristic of

Chapelain's manner that although he does not always take Scudéry's side, he often finds other reasons for criticism that had not been advanced in the *Observations*; and there can be no doubt that his more judicious approach results in a judgement that is just as hostile to *Le Cid*. The tone of the *Sentiments* can be assessed from this remark in the introductory section, in which Chapelain proposes to examine 'non pas tant si [la pièce] avait plu, mais si elle avait dû plaire' (p. 359). This reflects an uncompromisingly élitist critical stance, on the part of one who believes without question in the difference between untutored enthusiasm and the discerning appreciation of the trained mind: in seventeenth-century terms, between 'plaire' and 'plaire selon les règles'. Implicit in the approach of the discriminating playgoer is an understanding of the critical tradition inherited from the Ancients. The *Sentiments* are a key text in the formation of that 'doctrine classique' that was to dominate aesthetic thinking throughout the century; and however much Corneille himself was to be influenced by such thinking during the course of his career, he was always to remain, both temperamentally and empirically, something of a rebel, whose example was to be a principal inspiration of the modernists at the end of the century in the 'Querelle des anciens et des modernes'. The two main issues on which Chapelain takes a stand are the question of the moral utility of a work of art, and closely allied to this, the choice between 'le vrai' and 'le vraisemblable'. To claim that a play can give pleasure without being morally profitable, says Chapelain, is to accept a very low estimate of aesthetic pleasure: we must insist on 'un contentement raisonnable', and 'nous ne dirons pas sur la foi du peuple qu'un ouvrage de poésie soit bon parce qu'il l'aura contenté, si les doctes aussi n'en sont contents' (p. 360). The continuing love of Chimène for Rodrigue, and her agreement to marry him, are obviously a test case; and here the dramatist should have preferred the *vraisemblable* to the historically true:

> S'il est obligé de traiter une matière historique de cette nature, c'est alors qu'il la doit réduire aux termes de la bienséance,

> sans avoir égard à la vérité, et qu'il la doit plutôt changer tout
> entière que de lui laisser rien qui soit incompatible avec les
> règles de son art; lequel se proposant l'idée universelle des
> choses, les épure des défauts et des irrégularités particulières
> que l'histoire par la sévérité de ses lois est contrainte d'y
> souffrir.   (p. 366)

In the light of this general principle, Chapelain goes so far as
to propose alternative endings that Corneille might have
adopted, modifying the historical narrative in the interests of
bienséance. It could have been discovered at the denouement
that the Comte was not Chimène's real father; he might have
been found not to have died from his wounds; or it would
have been possible to invent an overwhelming political reason for Chimène's marriage to Rodrigue: 'que le salut du Roi
et du Royaume eût absolument dépendu de ce mariage, pour
compenser la violence que souffrait la nature en cette occasion par le bien que le Prince et son état en recevrait'. Any of
these expedients, says Chapelain, would have been preferable
to the unpalatable historical truth. But, he concludes with
magisterial sternness, 'le plus expédient eût été de n'en point
faire de poème dramatique, puisque [l'événement] était trop
bien connu pour l'altérer en un point si essentiel, et de trop
mauvais exemple pour l'exposer à la vue du peuple sans
l'avoir auparavant rectifié' (p. 366).

This damning judgement is the only logical conclusion
possible from Chapelain's premises. The author of the *Sentiments* seems to recognise that the expedients he proposes are
not really compatible with a serious and dignified approach
to historical subject-matter; and faced with a situation in
which he had no valid alternative to creating something that
would be morally unedifying, the dramatist should have
recognised this and chosen another subject. Particularly, of
course, since in the case of *Le Cid* the provocative character
of the historical subject itself was compounded by Corneille's
determination to treat it in regular form. Whereas Castro
had at least spread the action of his version over several days,
'le Français', says Chapelain, 'qui a voulu se renfermer dans
la règle des vingt-quatre heures, pour éviter une faute est

tombé dans une autre, et de crainte de pécher contre les règles de l'art, a mieux aimé pécher contre celles de la nature' (p. 370).

Chapelain's uncompromising stand on *vraisemblance* and the unities as the principles of regular drama was matched by an equally firm approach to linguistic usage. Here too, the *Sentiments* can be seen as pointing forward towards the mature classicism of the next generation: a *vraisemblable* subject, treated according to the rules, required simplicity and clarity of expression. Though they stop well short of the worst of Scudéry's hair-splitting (for instance on l. 1447: 'Sortir d'une bataille, et combattre à l'instant!', Scudéry comments: 'Ce combat des Maures, fait de nuit, n'était point une bataille', p. 102), Chapelain's own linguistic glosses are not always exempt from pedantry, and he makes little allowance for poetic licence. Commenting on l. 1715 (1637 ed.): 'Madame, à vos genoux j'apporte cette épée', he writes: 'On peut bien *apporter une épée aux pieds* de quelqu'un, mais non pas *aux genoux*' (p. 413); and l. 589: 'Commandez que son bras, nourri dans les alarmes...' is criticised because 'On ne peut dire, *un bras nourri dans les alarmes,* et [l'auteur] a mal pris en ce lieu la partie pour le tout' (p. 403). The ideals of clarity and linguistic purity are not achieved without some sacrifice of vigour and expressivity;[25] and Chapelain is, with Malherbe, one of the principal architects of an alexandrine which, for all its harmony, will need the genius of a Racine to keep it from lapsing into the prosaic and the banal.

The Academy's arbitration, from the pen of the scholarly Chapelain, was thus no more to Corneille's liking than Scudéry's personally motivated *Observations* had been. Chapelain's criticism, honest, if limited, picked on largely the same features of *Le Cid*; and the fact that Chapelain's tone was more measured must have made what he said all the more telling. However, side by side with their negative aspect – their dogmatic insistence on inflexible rationalistic criteria –

---

[25] In the case of the first of these examples Corneille took note of Chapelain's criticism, with the result that the revised version reads (l. 1705): 'Obligé d'apporter à vos pieds cette épée...'.

it could be said that the *Sentiments* offer, if not quite a complete blueprint for the neo-classical tragedy to which Corneille was to turn, at least a firm theoretical basis on which that tragedy could develop.

The effects of the Querelle on Corneille himself were threefold. First of all, it resulted in quite a long delay before his next play was offered to the public. In the seven years up to and including the first performance of *Le Cid* he had produced nine plays; now, he was to take over three years to mature and develop his subject before presenting *Horace* in the spring of 1640. There were even rumours that, having been so discouraged by the attacks on *Le Cid*, he had withdrawn from the theatre for good; Chapelain writes, in a letter to Balzac on 15 January 1639:

> Il ne fait plus rien, et Scudéry a du moins gagné cela, en le querellant, qu'il l'a rebuté du métier, et lui a tari sa veine. Je l'ai, autant que je l'ai pu, réchauffé et encouragé à se venger, et de Scudéry et de sa protectrice, en faisant quelque nouveau *Cid...* mais il n'y a pas moyen de l'y résoudre.

However, Corneille apparently began to work on *Horace* during that same year; and the second, and most tangible, influence of the Querelle is of course to be seen in the choice of subject and in its treatment: a simple plot from an impeccable source, the Roman historian Livy, treated in strict conformity with the unities as understood at the end of the 1630s. While *Horace* is no more 'regular' than *Le Cid*, from now on Corneille was to select the kind of subject that could be treated without violence to the notions of unity of time and place.

The third result of the *Cid* controversy became apparent only some years later: this was the change in Corneille's own thinking about the critical issues raised by the Querelle, which was revealed as he endeavoured, on the publication of successive editions of the play, to disguise the extent by which he had fallen short of the classical formula, by now so much more widely accepted.

On the other hand, whatever the motives may have been for the changes he introduced in an attempt to satisfy the aesthetic criteria of mid-century classicism, Corneille was not willing to give way to Chapelain on the underlying principle of the moral instruction contained in a work of art. His *Épître* to *Médée* (published in 1639) can in fact be seen as representing the playwright's firm and considered response on this issue:

> La peinture et la poésie ont cela de commun... que l'une fait souvent de beaux portraits d'une femme laide, et l'autre de belles imitations d'une action qu'il ne faut pas imiter. Dans la portraiture, il n'est pas question si un visage est beau, mais s'il ressemble; et dans la poésie, il ne faut pas considérer si les mœurs sont vertueuses, mais si elles sont pareilles à celles de la personne qu'elle introduit. Aussi nous décrit-elle indifféremment les bonnes et les mauvaises actions, sans nous proposer les dernières pour exemple... Il n'est pas besoin d'avertir ici le public que celles de cette tragédie ne sont pas à imiter: elles paraissent assez à découvert pour n'en faire envie à personne. Je n'examine point si elles sont vraisemblables ou non... il me suffit qu'elles sont autorisées ou par la vérité de l'histoire, ou par l'opinion commune des anciens.

On this fundamental point, we can observe a remarkable consistency in Corneille's theory and practice throughout his career (the question is admirably treated in *18*).

5

Le Cid from 1637 to 1660: Tragicomedy or Tragedy?

O N E thing should be clear from the study of the 1637 text of the final scene, and from what has been said about the principal contributions to the Querelle: that all parties seem to have taken for granted at that date that the play ended with Chimène's tacit agreement to marry Rodrigue in a year's time. The heroine's last protest, in its original form, is entirely concerned with the question of *immediate* marriage:

> Qu'un même jour commence et finisse mon deuil,
> Mette en mon lit Rodrigue et mon père au cercueil...

Reassured by the King's reply:

> Le temps assez souvent a rendu légitime
> Ce qui semblait d'abord ne se pouvoir sans crime...

she makes no further objection; and there was no valid reason in 1637 to regard the 'hymen différé' of the King's penultimate speech as anything other than a happy ending. And it was obviously in this light that it was seen by Scudéry and Chapelain, for at no point does either of these writers envisage the possibility of an alternative interpretation of the final scene. Chapelain may put forward his romanesque variants on the denouement as possible ways of reconciling the marriage with sound moral example, but it evidently did not occur to him to doubt that the marriage was intended to take place. Any more than it did to Corneille and his supporters: for what better rejoinder could there have been to the denunciation of Chimène as a 'fille dénaturée' for marrying her father's killer, than to argue that the marriage was not meant to take place – or at least that the play was intended to end inconclusively? Even Corneille, Norman lawyer though he was, made no attempt to justify himself in this way; and at the time of the Querelle his only response to accusations of immorality was to plead the guarantee of historical truth.

By 1682, the date of the definitive state of the text of *Le Cid,* in the four-volume *Théâtre de Corneille* (the last collective edition published by the poet himself), the situation had changed considerably. By 1648, the genre of tragicomedy was already out of fashion, and regular tragedy was well established in public favour, at least in Paris; in an edition published in that year, the play is first labelled 'tragédie' – though since this is also true of *Clitandre,* one should perhaps not make too much of what is possibly a pure formality. It was in this same edition of 1648 that Corneille first accompanied the text of his play with an 'Avertissement', in which he comments belatedly on the critical issues raised during the Querelle. This is a text characterised by common sense and judgement, showing neither the self-glorification nor the lawyer's logic-chopping which mark so much of Corneille's critical writing. On the subject of Aristotle's authority, he shows much more discernment than many a seventeenth-century writer, when he distinguishes between the fixed essentials of the aesthetic theory propounded in the *Poetics,* and the accessory details of form and structure that must always be subject to local variations. *Le Cid* owed its success, Corneille claims, to the fact that it satisfied the 'deux maîtresses conditions' posited by Aristotle:

> La première est que celui qui souffre et est persécuté ne soit ni tout méchant ni tout vertueux, mais un homme plus vertueux que méchant, qui par quelque trait de faiblesse humaine qui ne soit pas un crime, tombe dans un malheur qu'il ne mérite pas; l'autre, que la persécution et le péril ne viennent point d'un ennemi, ni d'un indifférent, mais d'une personne qui doive aimer celui qui souffre et en être aimée.

And with regard to the vexed question of Chimène's marriage, he makes it clear that he has not changed his mind: the marriage is justified because it is historically true, and Corneille quotes the authority of historical and literary texts to support his argument.

It is the three-volume *Théâtre de Corneille* of 1660 which introduces significant changes in Corneille's thinking about *Le Cid*: changes so significant that they force the reader to examine the whole question of genre in connection with this play. The important modification in the text of the play itself is confined to the substitution of these lines in Chimène's final speech (lines 1805-12 of the substantive version; cf. lines 1831-38 of the 1637 edition):

> Mais à quoi que déjà vous m'ayez condamnée,
> Pourrez-vous à vos yeux souffrir cet hyménée?
> Et quand de mon devoir vous voulez cet effort,
> Toute votre justice en est-elle d'accord?
> Si Rodrigue à l'état devient si nécessaire,
> De ce qu'il fait pour vous dois-je être le salaire,
> Et me livrer moi-même au reproche éternel
> D'avoir trempé mes mains dans le sang paternel?

The heroine's protest is no longer confined to the immediate conclusion of her marriage ('un même jour...'); she now objects, with no such qualification, to all thought of marriage to Rodrigue as an offence against natural justice. It is true that the King still counters this objection with the offer of a year's delay, and to that extent it could be argued that the denouement remains the same. On the other hand, 'Le temps assez souvent a rendu légitime / Ce qui semblait d'abord ne se pouvoir sans crime', as a reply to Chimène's speech, no longer has the same logical force; and that being so, the latter's assent can no longer be taken entirely for granted. Moreover, for confirmation of the extent to which Corneille's thinking has changed, we can refer to his own commentary, also published in the 1660 edition.

One difficulty in interpreting his new attitude is that this edition contains two texts relating to the denouement of *Le Cid,* and that these two texts contradict each other. A passage in the *Discours du poème dramatique* takes the opportunity of replying to the criticism that *Le Cid* and other plays are 'unfinished' because the principal characters do not marry 'au sortir du théâtre':

> A quoi il est aisé de répondre que le mariage n'est point un achèvement nécessaire pour la tragédie heureuse, ni même pour la comédie. Quant à la première, c'est le péril d'un héros qui la constitue, et lorsqu'il en est sorti, l'action est terminée. Bien qu'il ait de l'amour, il n'est point besoin qu'il parle d'épouser sa maîtresse quand la bienséance ne le permet pas; et il suffit d'en donner l'idée après en avoir levé tous les empêchements, sans lui en faire déterminer le jour. Ce serait une chose insupportable que Chimène en convînt avec Rodrigue dès le lendemain qu'il a tué son père...

Two points of interest are to be noted here: the use of the expression 'la tragédie heureuse', to which I shall return later; and second, the continuing assumption that the marriage between Rodrigue and Chimène will take place. The objection on grounds of *bienséance* is acknowledged, but is still adequately met by postponement of the marriage itself: 'il suffit d'en donner l'idée après en avoir levé tous les empêchements, sans lui en faire déterminer le jour'. However, a radically different conclusion is drawn in the *Examen,* where Corneille argues quite unequivocally that the play ends with no marriage being arranged or concluded. Not all of the points he makes are equally convincing. Thus, in the final scene, Chimène 'ne se tait qu'après que le Roi a différé [l'exécution de cette loi qui la donne à son amant], et lui a laissé lieu d'espérer qu'avec le temps il y pourra survenir quelque obstacle'. And even Chimène's silence is now pressed into service as an argument against her consent:

> Je sais bien que le silence passe d'ordinaire pour une marque de consentement; mais quand les rois parlent, c'en est une de contradiction: on ne manque jamais à leur applaudir quand on entre dans leurs sentiments; et le seul moyen de leur contredire avec le respect qui leur est dû, c'est de se taire...

But convincing or not, the sense of the new interpretation is undeniable; and even the historical guarantee of Chimène's consent to the marriage, by which Corneille had previously set such store, is now jettisoned:

> Il est vrai que dans ce sujet il faut se contenter de tirer Rodrigue de péril, sans le pousser jusqu'à son mariage avec Chimène. Il est historique, et a plu en son temps; mais bien sûrement il déplairait au nôtre; et j'ai peine à voir que Chimène y consente chez l'auteur espagnol, bien qu'il donne plus de trois ans de durée à la comédie qu'il en a faite. Pour ne pas contredire l'histoire, j'ai cru ne me pouvoir dispenser d'en jeter quelque idée, mais avec incertitude de l'effet; et ce n'était que par là que je pouvais accorder la bienséance du théâtre avec la vérité de l'événement. (*Examen*)

Whereas the passage from the *Discours* looks back to the text of 1637, the interpretation offered by the *Examen* corresponds to the text of Chimène's last speech as revised for the 1660 edition. We can, I think, be confident that the *Discours*, though published in the same 1660 edition, was composed at an earlier date than the *Examen*, and that the new interpretation reflects a comparatively late development in the author's ideas. It is a development that brings him into line with the ideas expressed by Scudéry and Chapelain at the time of the Querelle – but there is no need to look back to a twenty-year-old controversy to explain Corneille's volte-face. The aesthetic doctrine formulated by Corneille's critics during the Querelle had been crystallised more recently in *La Pratique du théâtre* by the abbé d'Aubignac (a protégé of Richelieu's, as we have seen, at the time of *Le Cid*); started in the early 1640s, this influential work had not been published until 1657, so that when Corneille came to revise his play, he must have been very conscious of the recent impact of the abbé's critical ideas, particularly his insistence on *le vraisemblable* as the only acceptable foundation of tragic drama. The only plausible explanation, as I see it, of the interpretation now advanced in the *Examen* is that it represents a tactical manœuvre. There is plenty of evidence that Corneille had not changed his mind about the choice between *le vrai* and *le vraisemblable*; but rather than risk a headlong confrontation with d'Aubignac at this stage, he seems to have found it more prudent to abandon his stand on *Le Cid*, a play which had in any case by 1660 become in other respects something of an anachronism.

6

Le Cid since Corneille's Day

T E X T U A L changes after 1660 are unimportant; as Maurice Cauchie writes: 'il n'y a réellement que deux *Cid*: le *Cid* de 1637, graduellement mais très peu modifié jusqu'en 1657, et le *Cid* de 1660, graduellement mais très peu modifié jusqu'en 1682' (*1*, p. iii). The emphasis given to the differences between the 1637 and the 1660 texts of the play varies considerably from one commentator to another; and there is by no means complete agreement, throughout the abundant literature on the subject, about the significance of these changes. There are those who play down, or ignore, the modifications introduced in 1660, and who are content to accept that the play ends happily: thus P. J. Yarrow (see *43*). H. C. Ault, on the contrary, while equally prepared to overlook the textual alterations, relies on a psychological understanding of Chimène's position to support his declaration that 'There can be no future for [Rodrigue and Chimène] save long weary years of loneliness and regret... Chimène was right: her father's death forever separates Rodrigue and her' (*12*, p. 167). Nadal, followed by Pocock, recognises the importance of the textual change in Chimène's last speech; but both draw from this evidence a conclusion that seems to be at variance with what the 1637 text actually says, in that they ignore the all-important temporal restriction ('Qu'un meme jour...'). Nadal comments that 'une variante (1637-56) soulignait cette impossibilité où se trouvait Chimène d'"épouser" Rodrigue – et nous entendons bien qu'il s'agit de mariage charnel, "mettant Rodrigue dans le lit de Chimène"' (*32*, p. 353) – an interpretation amplified in this commentary by Pocock:

> In the original text Chimène's last refusal to marry Rodrigue
> was more explicit and emphatic... the first version, with its
> firm antitheses and concrete language, stressed only too effec-
> tively the barriers between Rodrigue and Chimène, and Cor-
> neille, meaning to make plain they would marry, replaced it
> by the final version, with its more abstract language, its use of
> the interrogative and the conditional, its stress on Rodrigue's
> importance to the state, and its deference to the King. If he
> really intended us to think that the lovers are parted for ever
> (which is hard enough to read into the original text), it is
> strange that when he revised the play he made his intention
> even harder to recognise.   (*36,* pp. 34-35)

It should not be necessary to emphasise that such an interpretation of Corneille's intentions, even if it could be reconciled
with the text of the final scene, would still be belied by what
the playwright says in the *Examen.*

The first full and balanced assessment of all the relevant
evidence was presented by G. Couton in his little study
Réalités dans le Cid in 1953. Couton places a greater emphasis than any other critic on the radical changes in Corneille's
attitude that had preceded the 1660 edition. 'En 1660', he
does not hesitate to claim, 'la tragédie est remaniée jusqu'à
devenir un second *Cid'.* If the first version had a 'dénouement
à l'espagnole', the revised ending is a 'dénouement à la nor-
mande', suggests Couton (*20,* pp. 102, 120); and he does not
conceal the fact that the former, in his view, carries more
conviction. And indeed, there is every reason to judge the
1637 version the more successful, in terms of aesthetic coherence and consistency with the rest of the play. For in the
transition from 1637 to 1660, Corneille's heroine not only
takes on a greater psychological complexity; as R. Pintard
suggests, if she is 'moins simple', she also becomes 'moins
généreuse', so that 'le lecteur d'après 1660 qui la suit dans les
détours de sa dialectique trop ingénieuse est en droit de se
demander si sa ruse d'aujourd'hui ne prépare pas un revire-
ment plus tard' (*35,* p. 46).[26]

[26] For a recent review of the evidence concerning the denouement, see *23.*

In other words, the evolution from baroque tragicomedy to classical tragedy – the evolution which produced the series of masterpieces beginning with *Horace, Cinna* and *Polyeucte* – was not achieved in the case of *Le Cid* without a certain cost. For the plays composed in the aftermath of the Querelle du Cid, Corneille sought a simple subject, capable of being treated in strict conformity with the unities; and the relative paucity of incident enabled the dramatist to devote greater attention to the various reactions to each stage in the plot, and to examine the developing relationships between the principal characters in a more expansive way. In *Le Cid,* neither the new label of *tragédie* nor the token changes made to the text could disguise the fact that the subject had been chosen for a different style of writing: a baroque display of contrasting attitudes, attitudes which are determined by unforeseen external events to a degree not found in mature classical tragedy. Thus, to call *Le Cid* a 'tragedy' in 1648 was to identify it as something of a hybrid. It is not so much a question of the happy ending: Corneille was to favour what he called 'la tragédie heureuse' throughout his most fruitful creative period, from *Horace* in 1640 to *Pertharite* in 1653, and neither he nor his contemporaries saw anything incongruous between the optimistic conclusions of plays like *Cinna* or *Nicomède* and the status of such plays as tragedies. Subsuming this, however, is the whole question of the heroic, romanesque aesthetic of which *Le Cid* is the masterpiece: an aesthetic which put a premium on the virtuoso expression of emotion rather than on the sustained development of coherent character. And although some of this carries over into the aesthetic of *admiration* which Corneille will defend in the *Au Lecteur* to *Nicomède* of 1651, *Le Cid* was already being criticised in 1637 in the name of a more rationalistic approach to imaginative writing. Corneille's critics may not have been wholly clear – or entirely unanimous – about the direction in which they were leading the new drama; P. Martino says of d'Aubignac, for instance, that 'la tragédie qu'il rêve n'est pas la tragédie classique. Son idéal semble être plutôt une tragicomédie épurée, simplifiée, perfectionnée' (9, p. xxv). But even in the light of this modest programme, less demanding and less forward-looking than Chapelain's, *Le Cid* had been found wanting; and Corneille's own hesitations and contradictions suggest that by 1660 he had come round to his erstwhile opponents' way of thinking – at least to the extent of finding the baroque inspiration of his tragicomedies something of an embarrassment. However, to call *Le Cid* a tragedy, to modify some of the baroque flamboyance of the original text, even to cast doubt on the heroine's marriage as being not only contrary to *la bienséance,* but also failing to pass the test of psychological credibility: these were half-measures whose real effect is surely to emphasise the very different inspiration of the original version of 1637.

While Corneille was endeavouring to persuade his readers that *Le Cid* could be accommodated to the new formula of neo-classical tragedy, the play continued to be performed – at the Hôtel de Bourgogne and also by Molière's company (who first put it on in Paris in July 1659, shortly after their return from the provinces). It is safe to assume that by then any attempt to distinguish between the different locations (King's palace, Chimène's house, street) had been abandoned; and the adoption of a single set is formally recorded in this brief entry in the notebook of Michel Laurent, *décorateur* at the Hôtel de Bourgogne, dated by Lancaster at 1678:

> *Le Cid.* Théâtre est une chambre à quatre portes. Il faut un fauteuil pour le Roi. (*28,* p. 112)

'*Le Cid* est, de très loin, celle des tragédies de Corneille qui s'adapte le moins au décor unique', writes M. Descotes (*21,* p. 51). However, once fitted into the classical mould, in this respect as in others, the play was subjected to the standardising influence of official taste, and was produced in the equivalent of the Racinian 'palais à volonté' throughout the *ancien régime.* Seen in the light of this long-standing approach to the *mise en scène* of the play, therefore, the question we have considered briefly above – that of the location of Act V, scenes vi and vii – becomes of even more marginal relevance.

Accommodated, *tant bien que mal,* to the now universally
accepted classical canon, *Le Cid* had mixed fortunes in the
eighteenth century. The celebrated actor Baron was the link
with the past: trained by Molière, he had been the first
Rodrigue after the 'jonction des troupes' and the founding of
the Comédie-Française in 1680. Anecdotal history remem-
bers this actor above all in his later years, when he returned
to the theatre and was still playing Rodrigue and other *jeune
premier* roles well into his seventies: there are the familiar
stories of the audience's laughter at 'Je suis jeune, il est vrai...'
being turned into applause by the confidence and authority
with which he repeated the line, and of his kneeling at
Chimène's feet and being unable to rise. But as Descotes has
shown, there is enough evidence surviving to demonstrate
Baron's particular distinction: following Molière's precepts
for a natural, rather than a declamatory, manner of delivery,
he was of inestimable importance in determining the development of tragic acting in the eighteenth century; and the
role of Rodrigue was evidently central to this achievement
(see *21,* pp. 71-73). Later in the century, Lekain distinguished
himself in other Cornelian roles, but that of Rodrigue was not
one in which he felt at ease; nor, according to Descotes, did
Lecouvreur, Clairon or Dumesnil, the outstanding actresses
of the century, make their mark as Chimène. The play's
mixed reception in the theatre is mirrored in the critical
interpretation of the period, of which Voltaire's *Commentaires sur Corneille* are a typical example. Although Voltaire
pays homage to 'ce combat des passions qui déchire le cœur,
et devant lequel toutes les autres beautés de l'art ne sont que
des beautés inanimées', and although he is scornful of the
pedantic criticism of Scudéry and Chapelain, his own comments, not only on verbal expression and literary style but
also on the dramaturgical structure of the play, indicate
clearly enough that he is uneasy with a work of such hybrid
inspiration, in an age which increasingly looked back to the
masterpieces of the previous century above all as models of
refined taste and stylistic perfection (see *10,* Vol. 53, pp. 214 ff.;
Vol. 54, pp. 38 ff.).

In the nineteenth century, Corneille was enrolled in support of the Romantics' campaign against the neo-classical tragedy deriving from the examples of Racine and Voltaire: Corneille – and particularly the early Corneille of *Le Cid* – was somewhat tendentiously interpreted by Hugo and others as a playwright whose 'Spanish' temperament was stifled, and his creative talents deformed, by being forced to adopt the formula of regular tragedy. In the theatre, as a result of the more flexible critical approach proclaimed by the Romantics, and also of a better understanding of Shakespeare, certain *metteurs en scène* were prepared to challenge the long-standing tradition: a production at the Théâtre-Français in 1842, with Rachel as Chimène, for the first time reverted to changes of scene – but between the acts only, not in the middle of an act. [27] Since that date, experiment has been taken for granted in a continuing interaction between traditionalists and innovators – if one can label innovation the desire on André Antoine's part, for a production at the Odéon in 1907, to recapture the total visual effect of the original performances at the Marais, even down to the rows of spectators on stage. By general agreement, the most impressive of modern productions was that undertaken by Jean Vilar for the Théâtre National Populaire (Avignon 1949, Paris 1951), with Gérard Philipe as Rodrigue; as Descotes reports, 'Par des jeux de tentures et de lumière, écartant tout recours à des accessoires de style réaliste, Vilar ramena le problème du décor multiple à sa juste valeur, qui est secondaire' (*21,* p. 58).

What the T.N.P. production allowed to come through and to speak for itself, possibly more successfully than any other presentation of Corneille's play since Mondory's original staging, was the youthful enthusiasm, the spontaneous vitality, of the text, the blend of the heroic, the lyrical and the elegiac which had characterised the original creation. These

[27] It should be remembered that not only were Hugo's plays written according to the same convention (a single décor for the whole of each act), but even when Musset's *Lorenzaccio* was adapted for its first stage production as late as 1896, it was rearranged to fit this same formula.

qualities had been repressed by the theatrical conventions
governing *mise en scène* throughout nearly three centuries,
just as they had been depreciated by the conservative criticism of the academic establishment during most of the same
period.[28] One of the most striking things about Corneille
scholarship during this post-war period is the way in which
his early works have benefited from the new interest in the
history and culture of the baroque period as something justified for its own sake, and not as a prelude to the greater
glories of the 'Siècle de Louis XIV'. *Le Cid* in its turn has
been looked at in a new light, in a closer relationship both
with Corneille's own early plays and with those of his
contemporaries; and it can now be seen in its 1637 form, no
longer as an imperfect prototype of the versions of 1660 and
1682, but as a masterpiece in its own right. It has been the
aim of the present study to demonstrate the extent to which
Corneille's best-known play was shaped by the cultural cli-
mate in which it was first performed; and I hope I may
have succeeded in showing that a sympathetic appreciation of
Le Cid depends on the ability to recognise, behind 'la
première des tragédies classiques', the original tragicomedy of
1637.

Having said that, it is only proper to recognise that what
makes of *Le Cid* the outstanding masterpiece of baroque
tragicomedy is paradoxically the latent tension between the
old and the new: the fact that its author was not content with
the romanesque mould that had shaped a play like *Clitandre,*
whose chief attraction (apart from its engaging literary style)
had been a succession of bizarre and unexpected events. By
the time of *Le Cid* – partly no doubt owing to his apprentice-
ship in the creation of plausible, if unusual, characters in his
series of comedies up to *La Place Royale* – Corneille had
come to look for more than bizarre event; and even if he was
always to emphasise the *invraisemblable* in his search for a
dramatic subject, this was to be reconciled, in the aesthetic of

[28] Mention might be made in this context of Massenet's opera *Le Cid*
(1885), which succeeds admirably in capturing the 'pre-classical' heroics of
Corneille's play.

admiration which gives such an individual quality to his mature work, with greater psychological plausibility. When he composed *Le Cid,* he may not have been fully aware of the tension between the romanesque characteristics typical of tragicomedy and the psychological conviction that was beginning to be a distinctive feature of the new drama. One of the functions of the Querelle du Cid was to focus on that tension, and to influence the way in which Corneille would resolve it in the plays of the 1640s and 1650s; but we can see now that it was already present, whether consciously or not, in the mind of the playwright of 1636, and it is impossible to overestimate the importance of this creative tension in shaping the peculiar qualities of *Le Cid.*

Appendix

THE 1637 text of the scenes most affected by the changes introduced in the 1660 edition (and retained in that of 1682) is given here.

(a)   *Act I, scenes i-ii (1682, scene i):*

ACTE I

SCÈNE PREMIÈRE

LE COMTE, ELVIRE

ELVIRE

Entre tous ces amants dont la jeune ferveur
Adore votre fille et brigue ma faveur,
Don Rodrigue et Don Sanche à l'envi font paraître
Le beau feu qu'en leurs cœurs ses beautés ont fait naître.
5   Ce n'est pas que Chimène écoute leurs soupirs
Ou d'un regard propice anime leurs désirs:
Au contraire, pour tous dedans l'indifférence,
Elle n'ôte à pas un ni donne d'espérance,
Et, sans les voir d'un œil trop sévère ou trop doux,
10   C'est de votre seul choix qu'elle attend un époux.

LE COMTE

Elle est dans le devoir: tous deux sont dignes d'elle,
Tous deux formés d'un sang noble, vaillant, fidèle,
Jeunes, mais qui font lire aisément dans leurs yeux
L'éclatante vertu de leurs braves aïeux.

15 Don Rodrigue surtout n'a trait en son visage
    Qui d'un homme de cœur ne soit la haute image,
    Et sort d'une maison si féconde en guerriers,
    Qu'ils y prennent naissance au milieu des lauriers.
    La valeur de son père, en son temps sans pareille,
20 Tant qu'a duré sa force a passé pour merveille;
    Ses rides sur son front ont gravé ses exploits
    Et nous disent encor ce qu'il fut autrefois.
    Je me promets du fils ce que j'ai vu du père,
    Et ma fille, en un mot, peut l'aimer et me plaire.
25 Va l'en entretenir; mais, dans cet entretien,
    Cache mon sentiment et découvre le sien:
    Je veux qu'à mon retour nous en parlions ensemble;
    L'heure à présent m'appelle au conseil qui s'assemble:
    Le Roi doit à son fils choisir un Gouverneur,
30 Ou plutôt m'élever à ce haut rang d'honneur;
    Ce que pour lui mon bras chaque jour exécute
    Me défend de penser qu'aucun me le dispute.

SCÈNE SECONDE

CHIMÈNE, ELVIRE

ELVIRE, *seule*

Quelle douce nouvelle à ces jeunes amants!
Et que tout se dispose à leurs contentements!

CHIMÈNE

35 Eh bien, Elvire, enfin, que faut-il que j'espère?
    Que dois-je devenir, et que t'a dit mon père?

ELVIRE

Deux mots dont tous vos sens doivent être charmés:
Il estime Rodrigue autant que vous l'aimez.

CHIMÈNE

L'excès de ce bonheur me met en défiance;
40 Puis-je à de tels discours donner quelque croyance?

ELVIRE

Il passe bien plus outre: il approuve ses feux,
Et vous doit commander de répondre à ses vœux.
Jugez après cela, puisque tantôt son père,
Au sortir du Conseil, doit proposer l'affaire,
45 S'il pouvait avoir lieu de mieux prendre son temps,
Et si tous vos désirs seront bientôt contents.

CHIMÈNE

Il semble toutefois que mon âme troublée
Refuse cette joie et s'en trouve accablée.
Un moment donne au sort des visages divers,
50 Et dans ce grand bonheur je crains un grand revers.

ELVIRE

Vous verrez votre crainte heureusement déçue.

CHIMÈNE

Allons, quoi qu'il en soit, en attendre l'issue.

(b) *Act V, scene vii:*

SCÈNE SEPTIÈME

LE ROI, D. DIÈGUE, D. ARIAS, D. RODRIGUE, D. ALONSE,
D. SANCHE, L'INFANTE, CHIMÈNE, LÉONOR, ELVIRE

L'INFANTE

Sèche tes pleurs, Chimène, et reçois sans tristesse
1800 Ce généreux vainqueur des mains de ta Princesse.

D. RODRIGUE

Ne vous offensez point, Sire, si devant vous
Un respect amoureux me jette à ses genoux.
Je ne viens point ici demander ma conquête:
Je viens tout de nouveau vous apporter ma tête;

1805 Madame, mon amour n'emploiera point pour moi
      Ni la loi du combat ni le vouloir du Roi.
      Si tout ce qui s'est fait est trop peu pour un père,
      Dites par quels moyens il vous faut satisfaire.
      Faut-il combattre encor mille et mille rivaux,
1810 Aux deux bouts de la terre étendre mes travaux,
      Forcer moi seul un camp, mettre en fuite une armée,
      Des Héros fabuleux passer la renommée?
      Si mon crime par là se peut enfin laver,
      J'ose tout entreprendre et puis tout achever.
1815 Mais si ce fier honneur, toujours inexorable,
      Ne se peut apaiser sans la mort du coupable,
      N'armez plus contre moi le pouvoir des humains:
      Ma tête est à vos pieds, vengez-vous par vos mains;
      Vos mains seules ont droit de vaincre un invincible:
1820 Prenez une vengeance à tout autre impossible.
      Mais du moins que ma mort suffise à me punir:
      Ne me bannissez point de votre souvenir,
      Et, puisque mon trépas conserve votre gloire,
      Pour vous en revancher conservez ma mémoire,
1825 Et dites quelquefois, en songeant à mon sort:
      "S'il ne m'avait aimée, il ne serait pas mort".

                              CHIMÈNE

      Relève-toi, Rodrigue. Il faut l'avouer, Sire,
      Mon amour a paru: je ne m'en puis dédire.
      Rodrigue a des vertus que je ne puis haïr,
1830 Et vous êtes mon Roi: je vous dois obéir.
      Mais, à quoi que déjà vous m'ayez condamnée,
      Sire, quelle apparence, à ce triste Hyménée,
      Qu'un même jour commence et finisse mon deuil,
      Mette en mon lit Rodrigue et mon père au cercueil?
1835 C'est trop d'intelligence avec son homicide,
      Vers ses Mânes sacrés c'est me rendre perfide
      Et souiller mon honneur d'un reproche éternel
      D'avoir trempé mes mains dans le sang paternel.

Le Roi

Le temps assez souvent a rendu légitime
1840   Ce qui semblait d'abord ne se pouvoir sans crime.
Rodrigue t'a gagnée, et tu dois être à lui;
Mais, quoique sa valeur t'ait conquise aujourd'hui,
Il faudrait que je fusse ennemi de ta gloire
Pour lui donner sitôt le prix de sa victoire.
1845   Cet Hymen différé ne rompt point une loi
Qui, sans marquer de temps, lui destine ta foi:
Prends un an si tu veux pour essuyer tes larmes.
Rodrigue, cependant il faut prendre les armes:
Après avoir vaincu les Mores sur nos bords,
1850   Renversé leurs desseins, repoussé leurs efforts,
Va jusqu'en leur pays leur reporter la guerre,
Commander mon armée et ravager leur terre.
A ce seul nom de Cid ils trembleront d'effroi;
Ils t'ont nommé Seigneur et te voudront pour Roi.
1855   Mais parmi tes hauts faits, sois-lui toujours fidèle;
Reviens-en, s'il se peut, encor plus digne d'elle,
Et par tes grands exploits fais-toi si bien priser,
Qu'il lui soit glorieux alors de t'épouser.

D. Rodrigue

Pour posséder Chimène et pour votre service,
1860   Que peut-on m'ordonner que mon bras n'accomplisse?
Quoi qu'absent de ses yeux il me faille endurer,
Sire, ce m'est trop d'heur de pouvoir espérer.

Le Roi

Espère en ton courage, espère en ma promesse,
Et, possédant déjà le cœur de ta maîtresse,
1865   Pour vaincre un point d'honneur qui combat contre toi
Laisse faire le temps, ta vaillance et ton Roi.

Fin du Cinquième et dernier Acte.

Bibliography

I. TEXTS

Works by Corneille

1. *Le Cid, tragicomédie,* édition originale, publiée avec notes et variantes par Maurice Cauchie, Paris, Didier (Société des Textes Français Modernes), 1946. (Text of 1637.)
2. *Le Cid, tragicomédie,* edited with an introduction and notes by Peter H. Nurse, London, Harrap, 1978. (Text of 1637.) Re-issued Oxford, Blackwell, 1988.
3. *Le Cid, tragédie,* avec une notice, etc. par Georges Griffe, Paris, Bordas (Univers des Lettres), 1962. (Text of 1682.)
4. *Œuvres,* ed. Georges Couton, Paris, Gallimard (Bibliothèque de la Pléiade), Vol. I, 1980.
5. *Trois discours sur le poème dramatique,* ed. L. Forestier, Paris, S.E.D.E.S., 1963.
6. *Writings on the Theatre,* edited by H. T. Barnwell, Oxford, Blackwell, 1965.

Works by Other Authors

7. J. Chapelain, *Les Sentiments de l'Académie Française sur la tragicomédie du Cid,* ed. G. Collas, Paris, Picard, 1912 (reprinted Geneva, Slatkine, 1968).
8. (various), *La Querelle du Cid, pièces et pamphlets,* ed. A. Gasté, Paris, Welter, 1898 (reprinted Geneva, Slatkine, 1970).
9. F. H. d'Aubignac, *La Pratique du théâtre,* ed. P. Martino, Paris, Champion, 1927.
10. Voltaire, *Commentaires sur Corneille,* ed. D. Williams (The Complete Works of Voltaire, Vols 53-55), Banbury, The Voltaire Foundation, 1974.

II. HISTORICAL AND CRITICAL WORKS

11. A. Adam, *Histoire de la littérature française au XVIIe siècle,* 5 vols, Paris, Domat, 1948-56.
12. H. C. Ault, 'The Tragic Genius of Corneille', *Modern Language Review,* 45 (1950), 164-76.

13. H. C. Ault, 'The Denouement of *Le Cid*: a further note', *Modern Language Review,* 48 (1953), 54-56.

14. H. T. Barnwell, *The Tragic Drama of Corneille and Racine: an old parallel revisited,* Oxford, Clarendon Press, 1982.

15. L. Batiffol, *Richelieu et Corneille: la légende de la persécution de l'auteur du Cid,* Paris, Calmann-Lévy, 1936.

16. P. Bénichou, *Morales du Grand Siècle,* Paris, Gallimard, 1948.

17. G. Brereton, *French Tragic Drama in the Sixteenth and Seventeenth Centuries,* London, Methuen, 1973.

18. D. R. Clarke, 'Corneille's Differences with the Seventeenth-Century Doctrinaires over the Moral Authority of the Poet', *Modern Language Review,* 80 (1985), 550-62.

19. G. Collas, 'Richelieu et *Le Cid'*, *Revue d'Histoire Littéraire de la France,* 43 (1936), 568-72.

20. G. Couton, *Réalisme de Corneille (La Clef de Mélite; Réalités dans le Cid),* Paris, Belles Lettres, 1953.

21. M. Descotes, *Les Grands Rôles du théâtre de Corneille,* Paris, P.U.F., 1962.

22. J. Golder, 'The Stage Settings of Corneille's Early Plays', *Seventeenth-Century French Studies,* 7 (1985), 184-97.

23. C. J. Gossip, 'The Denouement of *Le Cid*, yet again', *Modern Language Review,* 75 (1980), 275-81.

24. M. F. Hilgar, *La Mode des stances dans le théâtre tragique français, 1610-1687,* Paris, Nizet, 1974.

25. W. D. Howarth, 'Mécénat et raison d'état: Richelieu, Corneille et la tragédie politique' in *L'Age d'or du mécénat, 1598-1661,* Paris, C.N.R.S., 1985, pp. 59-68.

26. L. Lacour, *Richelieu dramaturge et ses collaborateurs,* Paris, Ollendorff, n.d. (c. 1925).

27. H. C. Lancaster, *A History of French Dramatic Literature in the Seventeenth Century,* 10 vols, Baltimore, Johns Hopkins U.P., 1929-42.

28. ed. H. C. Lancaster, *Le Mémoire de Mahelot, Laurent et d'autres décorateurs,* Paris, Champion, 1920.

29. J. Lough, *Paris Theatre Audiences in the Seventeenth and Eighteenth Centuries,* London, O.U.P., 1957.

30. M. Margitić, *Essai sur la mythologie du Cid,* University (Miss.), Romance Monographs, 1976.

31. G. Mongrédien, *Recueil des textes et des documents du XVIIe siècle relatifs à Corneille,* Paris, C.N.R.S., 1972.

32. O. Nadal, *Le Sentiment de l'amour dans l'œuvre de P. Corneille,* Paris, Gallimard, 1948.

33. ———, 'L'Ethique de la gloire et la société française', *Mercure de France,* 308 (1950), 22-34.

34. R. J. Nelson, *Corneille: his heroes and their worlds,* Philadelphia, Pennsylvania U.P., 1963.

35. R. Pintard, 'De la tragicomédie à la tragédie: l'exemple du *Cid'* in *Missions et démarches de la critique: mélanges offerts au professeur J. A. Vier,* Paris, Klincksieck, 1973.

36. G. Pocock, *Corneille and Racine: problems of tragic form,* Cambridge, C.U.P., 1973.
37. G. Reynier, *Le Cid de Corneille: étude et analyse,* Paris, Mellottée, 1929.
38. M. Sakharoff, *Le Héros, sa liberté et son efficacité, de Garnier à Rotrou,* Paris, Nizet, 1967.
39. J. Scherer, *La Dramaturgie classique en France,* Paris, Nizet, n.d. (1950).
40. W. L. Schwarz and C. B. Olsen, *The Sententiae in the Dramas of Corneille,* Stanford (Calif.), U.P., 1939.
41. W. L. Wiley, *The Early Public Theatre in France,* Cambridge (Mass.), Harvard U.P., 1960.
42. P. J. Yarrow, *Corneille,* London, Macmillan, 1963.
43. ———, 'The Denouement of *Le Cid*', *Modern Language Review,* 50 (1955), 270-73.

CRITICAL GUIDES TO FRENCH TEXTS

edited by

Roger Little, Wolfgang van Emden, David Williams